It is one of the best publications I have seen on the topic. I would be honored to recommend it highly for anybody who has the courage to delve into the issue of death and dying.

ELISABETH KÜBLER-ROSS, M.D.

With passion, creativity, and infinite sensitivity, David Feinstein and Peg Elliott Mayo have fashioned rituals and rites of passage that nurture relationships, ease transitions, and feed the spirit. Plumbed from the realms of living experience, this brilliant book will be appreciated by all who seek richness and meaning in difficult times.

JEANNE ACHTERBERG, PH.D.

A powerful step toward opening the mind to the heart . . . I would recommend this book to anyone confronting the grief of illness or loss.

STEPHEN LEVINE

The provocative exercises and the thoughtful text can help you approach death, and thus life, with enhanced integrity.

RAM DASS

Rituals for Living and Dying is a compassionate manual and useful preparation for those confronting death as well as for those actively seeking a richer life.

DAN MILLMAN

Building upon the fact that facing death frequently leads to a deepened connection with one's spiritual foundations, the authors offer a series of brilliantly crafted exercises for imaginatively grappling with the facts of life and death. The power, ingenuity, and depth of these structured experiences distinguish the work as unique in its field. The book is also wise and humorous, sad and uplifting, captivating and helpful.

STANLEY KRIPPNER, PH.D.

MORTAL ACTS

ALSO BY DAVID FEINSTEIN

Personal Mythology:
The Psychology of Your Evolving Self
(with Stanley Krippner)

The Many Faces of Eve:
A Mythic Journey Revisited
*(with Chris Costner Sizemore
and Stanley Krippner;* forthcoming)

ALSO BY PEG ELLIOTT MAYO

Blind Raftery:
Seven Nights of a Wake

Heroes in the Seaweed:
A Therapist's View of the Resilient Human Spirit

The Wild Soul Commentary:
Finding Our Way Home

MORTAL ACTS

Eighteen Empowering Rituals for Confronting Death

DAVID FEINSTEIN *and*
PEG ELLIOTT MAYO

An abridged and revised version
of *Rituals for Living and Dying*

HarperSanFrancisco
A Division of HarperCollins*Publishers*

MORTAL ACTS: *Eighteen Empowering Rituals for Confronting Death.* Copyright © 1993 by David Feinstein and Peg Elliott Mayo. All rights reserved. Printed in the United States of America. No part of this book may be used or reproduced in any manner whatsoever without written permission except in the case of brief quotations embodied in critical articles and reviews. For information address HarperCollins Publishers, 10 East 53rd Street, New York, NY 10022.

Originally published as part of *Rituals for Living and Dying* by HarperCollins in 1990.

FIRST HARPERCOLLINS PAPERBACK EDITION PUBLISHED IN 1993

Library of Congress Cataloging-in-Publication Data
Feinstein, David.
  Mortal acts : eighteen empowering rituals for confronting
death / David Feinstein and Peg Elliott Mayo. — 1st
HarperCollins pbk. ed.
    p.   cm.
"An abridged and revised version of Rituals for living and
dying."
Includes bibliographical references and index.
ISBN 0–06–250330–8 (pbk. : alk. paper)
1. Death—Psychological aspects. 2. Mythology—Psychological
aspects. 3. Rites and ceremonies. 4. Spiritual life. I. Mayo,
Peg Elliott. II. Feinstein, David. Rituals for living and dying.
III. Title
BF789.D4F455   1993
155.9'37—dc20   91–58905
                                                    CIP

93 94 95 96 97 ❖ CWI 9 8 7 6 5 4 3 2 1

This edition is printed on acid-free paper that meets the American National Standards Institute Z39.48 Standard.

For Patrick—he'd be so amazed!

And in loving memory of Fred—
Garnet's husband and Donna's father—who taught us so much
about courage, laughter, and learning how to see.

. . . all we can do
is now to be willing to die, and to build the ship
of death to carry the soul on the longest journey.

D. H. LAWRENCE, "The Ship of Death"

Contents

Preface

When we come into greater peace and understanding about death, we increase our capacity to live fully. Spiritual systems extending back to the beginning of human history have used the reality of death as a reflecting point in opening people to grace and harmony with nature. But whether you are just waking to the hardest facts of life and death or are already sensing the breath of mortality on your shoulders, you live in a society that is primitive in the ways in which it prepares its members to meet the emotional and spiritual challenges faced by the dying. According to Stanislav and Christina Grof:

> The individual dying in an ancient or pre-industrial culture is . . . equipped with a religious or philosophical system that transcends death, and is likely to have had considerable experiential training in altered states of consciousness, including symbolic confrontations with death. The approach of death is faced in the nourishing context of the extended family, clan, or tribe, and with its support—sometimes even with specific and expert guidance through the successive stages of dying. The situation of an average Westerner facing death is in sharp contrast to the above in every respect . . . "[1]

Mortal Acts is offered as a resource for addressing this impoverished area of our culture. It presents a systematic program for consciously and constructively addressing death. By encouraging an ambitious, mind-stretching exploration of personal mortality, it enhances our ability to live with the never-ending changes and mounting losses implicit in the world today. People everywhere are struggling to retain hope in an age in which every value and security is threatened. In coming to terms with our mortality, we create an aptitude for facing all other losses. Cultivating effective inner preparation for death—no matter what our current circumstances may be—prepares us for life's "little deaths": loss of purpose, status, security, relationship, opportunity. Without the capacity to adapt to loss, grief turns into self-pity rather than wisdom, fear to denial or panic rather than discernment, and anger to disempowering rage rather than effective action. The topic of this book is of compelling importance. Beyond reducing fear and anxiety, a serene acceptance of death brings a deep freedom that opens our hearts to greater love, joy, and gratitude.

This work is abridged and adapted from *Rituals for Living and Dying,* which presents separate programs for facing death and facing bereavement. *Mortal Acts* is based on the first of these programs, which was titled "Cultivating an Empowering Mythology for Confronting Death." Mythological thinking is rooted in the human capacity to symbolically address large questions, and cultivating an empowering mythology for confronting death addresses one of the largest questions that can be posed. Working with one's mythology on a core issue like death is a monumental and empowering undertaking: it is through the evolution of its mythologies, not its genes, that the human species now moves forward. The *personal mythology*—the deep beliefs, guiding images, and unspoken rules—we hold about living and dying exerts an invisible but decisive influence on the choices we make every day of our lives.

Cultural myths have always been conveyed, updated, and reinforced through the ancient intuitive art of ritual. *Mortal Acts* will guide you in a series of *personal* rituals for finding strength and tranquility in the face of inevitable physical death and the fears associated with the great unknown. Ritual forms occur across time and geography, uniting humankind through all the great themes of life: birth, maturation, bonding, decline, and death. By providing a sanctified framework within which spontaneous action and insight may occur, ritual can anchor us in the wisdom of time-honored traditions while encouraging us to take inventive steps attuned to contemporary life.

Cultural rituals extend to the individual a society's deepest wisdom for understanding events and facing life's passages, as in puberty rites that once taught boys the survival skills required of a hunter. *Personal* rituals, in our use of the term, lead people to their deepest *inner* wisdom for accessing guidance about core issues in their lives. In our work as therapists, we will frequently, during a session, find ourselves inventing a personal ritual designed to provide a client with an experience that will result in a discovery about an inner truth, a truth that shows the person how to make wiser choices. For example, in working with a man who cannot control his anger toward his wife, we may psychodramatically re-create his family of origin and design an "emotionally corrective experience" whereby he works through unresolved conflicts about anger, control, and aggression. By focusing on death, the personal rituals in this program are likely to provoke strong responses, ranging from fear and grief to spiritual longing to gratitude for the gift of life. These rituals offer a structure for working through fear and grief, for tapping into an inner wisdom about the meaning of death, for allowing your priorities to be affected by the fact that you are mortal, and for cultivating an understanding of death that brings you greater peace and inner strength.

These rituals challenge old myths and generate new visions. They expand your consciousness by bringing you to the edges of your existence, and they use death as the background in highlighting the possibilities for living more fully. The program has received strong and consistent feedback about the comfort and understanding it has generated in those who have used it, ranging from individuals wrestling with a life-threatening illness to people in a midlife crisis to medical professionals and hospice volunteers who went through the program as part of their training.

With this volume you will touch your mortality, examine the mythology you have developed to come to terms with it, and be challenged to cultivate an understanding of death that is purposeful, life-affirming, and likely to bring out the best in you. Rather than a morbid process, the excursion can enrich daily life and provide comfort in difficult times. In noting the "one important message" she hoped her book *Death: The Final Stage of Growth* would convey, Elisabeth Kübler-Ross stated, "Death does not have to be a catastrophic, destructive thing; indeed it can be viewed as one of the most constructive, positive, and creative elements of culture and life."[2] As you become more peaceful with your mortality, a deepened sense of purpose, a new level of self-possession, and a more profound connection with others may begin to unfold.

Our appreciations with respect to this project are many. First, we are indebted to the hundreds of clients who have opened themselves to us deeply during a combined half century of clinical practice and whose struggles, realizations, and achievements have afforded us a privileged view of the human journey. Names and details regarding those who serve as our case examples have, unless otherwise noted, been carefully disguised to conceal identities. Second, our gratitude for Stanley Krippner's wise counsel and generous support cannot be overstated. We are also deeply appreciative of the literally hundreds of constructive suggestions Ana Trelstad offered in her meticulous readings of the evolving manuscript. And it is a great joy to acknowledge our spouses—Donna and Don—who are not only friends with one another in their own right but are also marvelously tolerant of us: we thank them for their powerful support in birthing *Mortal Acts*.

Introduction

Death is a mirror in which the entire
meaning of life is reflected.[1]

The knowledge that death is approaching may have the para-
doxical effect of mobilizing a person into a more profound sense of
being alive. Two years after a near-fatal heart attack, Abraham
Maslow, one of this century's greatest psychologists, spoke of the
intervening period as "the postmortem life." Reflecting on how these
years were a kind of bonus, an extra gift, he noted that "if you're
reconciled with death or even if you are pretty well assured that you
will have a good death, a dignified one, then every single moment
of every single day is transformed because the pervasive undercur-
rent—the fear of death—is removed." In the postmortem life

> everything gets doubly precious, gets piercingly important.
> You get stabbed by things, by flowers and by babies and by
> beautiful things—just the very act of living, of walking and
> breathing and eating and having friends and chatting.
> Everything seems to look more beautiful rather than less, and
> one gets the much-intensified sense of miracles. . . . The con-
> frontation with death—and the reprieve from it—makes
> everything look so precious, so sacred, so beautiful that I feel
> more strongly than ever the impulse to love it, to embrace it,
> and to let myself be overwhelmed by it.[2]

People who, like Maslow, come into peace with the inevitability
of death are apt to find that life becomes sweeter. This paradox holds
a comforting twist. Even if they don't reach serenity about death
until the last few years of life, as did Maslow, or until the last few

days (and clinical evidence bears this out),[3] as they do attain it, they attain, in retrospect, new meaning for the lives they have lived. But why delay in finding peace about death and the renewed vitality that attends it?

ADVERSITY AND THE REBIRTH OF SPIRIT

Charles Cameron was sixty-seven when his world unraveled. Within a six-month period, he discovered that he had diabetes, his company required that he retire (a step he'd wanted to postpone for another three years), and his wife of forty-four years died in a plane crash. He became despairing and suicidal.

Never a religious person, Charles had no emotional, intellectual, or spiritual framework into which he could fit his losses. His life had comprised his work but, as he said later, "not much else." Stripped of his occupation as a sales executive for a pump-manufacturing firm, his humdrum but amicable marriage, and what had seemed good health, he saw no reason to live. It was only at the insistence of his grown son that he grudgingly agreed to enter psychotherapy. Charles said he had "abandoned hope and was just going through my paces to satisfy Danny. I really *wanted* to die, but I was also afraid of dying."

Charles's first task in therapy was to grieve his losses—professional identity, a secure and ordered marriage, and what felt like "the best years of my life—they're all behind me." It took him nearly a year of therapy to see beyond his pained confusion and come to a reluctant awareness that, with proper care, he might well live another twenty years. Initially, this seemed a gloomy prospect: "All I could imagine was a life of insulin shots, waning strength, dutiful dinner invitations from the kids, and television."

At this time Charles was in a serious automobile accident. Six weeks later, we asked him to describe his experience. He said, "I was on my way back from our mountain cabin—I was getting ready to put the place on the market—when it happened. I took a curve a little too fast—thinking about Margie and the good times we'd had up there.

"The next thing, I was airborne, and I saw the world tilt. I don't know how long it was, but when I came to, I was hanging upside down by the seat belt, and my head hurt like hell. I was cold, and it was getting dark. Everything in the car had shifted around, and I couldn't undo the buckle. The headlights were on, but I couldn't reach the horn—I was more scared than I've ever been in my life.

"I passed out, probably from all the blood rushing to my head, but I didn't pass out completely, if you know what I mean—kind of in and out. Like I knew where I was and that I was probably going to die in this grotesque way, but part of me felt sort of separated from it, too. Pretty soon the separated part began to turn away, to disconnect. Then I began to look around. It was a beautiful place—deep woods, river in the canyon, and a full moon coming over the ridge. And I noticed it was sort of misty—foggy—and I was just drifting over the forest floor. I didn't seem to have any substance, and the wind was moving me.

"Then came the moment I realized—but deeper than words—that *I am part of it all!* Even though I now believe I had literally died, I knew I didn't want to leave until I made friends with the planet again. I remembered being a kid and reveling in nature, and I knew I had to touch that again before I'd be ready to die. And I knew that something was holding it all together—all the pieces. I was irresistibly drawn to finding out more about what that was.

"I came to, still upside down, but I was thinking better. I squirmed around and got the seat belt unfastened. Then I crawled out of the passenger window and up the bank, and the first car along saw me.

"For a week I just basically sat and thought about what had happened. Actually, it wasn't *thought*—I sat and absorbed the experience. There never was any doubt about its reality, but what did it mean? Sally [his daughter-in-law] was a big help.

"She's interested in all that 'woo-woo' stuff like the *I Ching*, Tarot, and crystals. She told me that she was reading an article in one of her magazines that reminded her of my accident. It talked about a Tarot card called 'the Hanged Man,' and she read a passage to me:

The card represents surrender to death and resurrection as the soul leaves the body and then returns. Personality is torn away, and a higher power takes over. In the card, a man is pictured hanging upside down, attached to the tree by a snake, a symbol of wisdom. Energy rushes to the head, stimulating greater awareness. In his limited and precarious position, his only task is that of fighting for his life. While he struggles, all of his old realities drop away. He moves into a state of non-ordinary reality where anything is possible, where freedom and enlightenment reside. The boundaries between life and death blur and, if the initiation is successful, the initiate realizes that death is part of life. He then realizes the importance of living life fully and with passion.[4]

"Blew my mind! These words described exactly my experience hanging there in that car, and they gave form to my deepest inklings about the meaning of the experience. In the following weeks, it was as if the walls fell outward and I could explore ideas and feelings in a new way. A sense of peace came over me that I could not remember having had since I was a boy hiking in the Sierra Nevada. But I also had a sense of urgency. I wanted to drink up the richness of life I saw all around me. I started hiking again, and on every hike I've seen stunning sights I will never forget. I've also been taking much pleasure in reading John Muir's nature journals. The greatest joy comes from my children and, particularly, I must admit, my grandchildren. I was always proud of them, but I never slowed down enough to really let myself know them. Now I can enter their world, and it is the most extraordinary privilege I've ever had. I can speak with them in their own language and begin to teach them some of the lessons I've garnered in my own life. I hope I will be around long enough to see them into their own marriages and children, but even if I'm not, I think I'm planting the best guidance I have right into their foundations."

Coming to the brink of our mortality is usually terrifying. On the one hand, we tend to push away such dreadful proof of our vulnerability as quickly as possible. We cannot, after all, live effectively if we are endlessly focused on the precariousness of life. On the other hand, if we face the underlying anxiety and at the same time learn to accept our mortality, as did Charles Cameron, we invite a rebirth of spirit.

Somewhere in the process, the instinctual terror of death is likely to explode within us. To successfully move through it is to conquer a large measure of the nameless anxiety that we, individually and as a culture, exert so much effort to keep out of our minds.[5] When we have effectively squared off and faced that anxiety, we reclaim our misplaced energy. Less encumbered by nameless fears, we engage life with new vitality. This transformation is, however, a formidable challenge, and our culture provides few rites of passage to help us through it.

PERSONAL RITUALS AND RITES OF PASSAGE

"Illness," observed Marcel Proust, "is the most heeded of doctors—to goodness and wisdom we only make promises; we obey pain."[6] And fear. The inner strength and renewed vigor that proved to be the fruits of Charles Cameron's life crisis were harvested within a field of emotional pain. Pain and the fear of pain are certainly among nature's primary markers for guiding behavior and directing growth. Pain is an emphatic critic and teacher, but it is not the only teacher along the way.

Rituals and rites of passage are social inventions that once guided the human spirit on its journey through the world. The culture's wisdom was etched into the mind and body of every person participating in its rituals. Today, the lack of unity and coherence in the culture's mythic guidance allows and, in fact, forces people to think and act for themselves in ways that were unimaginable in the past. Major shifts in the culture's mythology—regarding issues as vital as what it means to be a man, a woman, a parent, a good citizen, a success—are being hammered out on the anvil of individual lives. Even what it means to die, once insistently established by religious canon, is left for each individual to puzzle through. We encounter these challenges without, for the most part, the benefit of sturdy tradition, inspiring myth, or vital ritual. Meanwhile, we are collectively starving for wise guidance attuned to the unique needs of the day—able to support the emphatic individuality that so strongly characterizes the modern psyche while promoting greater community and connection with the cosmos.[7] Dare we, unschooled and tentative, take on the task of reanimating myth and ritual as integral parts of our own lives?

Over the past century, the field of psychotherapy has cultivated a range of potent techniques for constructively intervening in the human psyche. These practices are relevant not only for treating psychopathology; they are also increasingly being used in helping people navigate the developmental crises of life that were once addressed by rites of passage and the mythic wisdom they carried. A strong confluence has been occurring in recent decades between increasingly powerful and precise therapeutic methods and the human need for ritual guidance.[8] Consider the following case history.

Carla Meadows struggled alone most of her life with a haunting fear of dirtying her hands, particularly with anything sticky. Over the years her concern grew, steadily and subtly, into a fear about touching such common items as doorknobs, money, plants, other people, or even her own outer clothing. A thirty-five-year-old graphic artist when she entered therapy, Carla was experiencing increasing misery. Simple household tasks required the use of rubber gloves, meticulous handwashing, obsessive arrangement of soaps and brushes, and immaculate towels at every sink in her home. Her concerns about "filth" had influenced her against having children: changing diapers was an idea she described as "the ultimate horror."

Carla knew she was "in trouble" when she could not leave home without her "kit." The kit, a small overnight case, held a plastic-wrapped towel, liquid surgical soap, a nail brush, and a two-quart container of filtered water. She entered therapy, reluctant and afraid of being labeled "crazy."

Compulsive phobic behavior is a spontaneous expression of the human need to exert a measure of control over the dangers and imponderables of life. We all need shelter in a dangerous world. Carla's reality was infused with sinister, invisible forces threatening to invade and destroy her. Every newscast, publication, and casual conversation reinforced her fear of powerful, invisible, malignant bacterial entities prowling the world and waiting in ambush to "get on my hands, stick to me, and get inside to hurt and maybe kill me."

Carla's compulsions were the culmination of several influences. Her mother was also a "clean freak" who scrubbed the woodwork so often it needed repainting every few months. Absolute about the importance of cleanliness, she had reacted with disgust when Carla, as a small child, became dirty in any way.

A second influence was the at-home death by diabetic gangrene of a beloved uncle. The attendant odors, dressings, and misery deeply reinforced Carla's mother's teachings and filled the watching child with vivid images. There was no effective memorial service or ritual for cleansing the house; rather, the older woman frantically disinfected and scrubbed the death room for years after his death. Trained by her mother in obsessive dread and ineffectual remedies, Carla reflected, "I guess I caught my fear from her." Carla's phobias and compulsions impeded intimate relationships and intensified in the years of isolation. Nor had Carla developed any spiritual framework for understanding her purpose in life or for coming to terms with her own mortality, a reality that she was frantically attempting to avert.

In therapy, Carla vividly described her view of the world: filth lurking everywhere; ugly, invisible invaders held at bay only through eternal vigilance and unremitting effort. She shared a recurrent dream that typified her fears. The dominant figure in the dream was a nasty, viral "germ," an evil invader capable of causing her to smell bad, feel awful, be dependent, and die hideously. Her therapist focused on these deeply held concepts and visions and set about assisting her to cultivate alternative images. One day, for instance, he brought a book with exquisitely colored illustrations of microscopic life into one of her therapy sessions. After Carla's initial repulsion at the idea of "bugs," the therapist helped her begin to appreciate the astounding beauty of the photographs.

Having shared her secret obsessive life with the therapist and having been met with understanding and concern, Carla began to trust and open to him as she had to no one else in her adult life. Now that she was no longer alone, her phobias and compulsions relaxed to some degree, plateauing at about the level they had been ten years earlier. The therapist believed that in order to get beyond this impasse, Carla would have to deal with the relentless echoes of her mother's fears reverberating in her psyche and with the scars left by her uncle's death. Indelible images of her uncle's illness haunted her any time she would willfully attempt to let up on her compulsive cleaning practices. The memory was so filled with horror that she had never attempted to examine it.

The therapist gave Carla the assignment of interviewing family members to find out as much as she could about her uncle and his life, of researching the medical facts about diabetic gangrene, and of preparing a eulogy for her uncle. She was also asked to procure, if possible, a personal item her uncle had used during the time he was ill. Her cousin, the uncle's son, was willing to part with an "L.A. Rams" coffee mug that his father always drank from during the last decade of his life, including the period of his illness. One of her therapy sessions was designated as a memorial service for her uncle. Held in a park, the uncle's picture was prominently displayed as Carla talked not only of the life he had lived and its meaning and of the nature of the illness that caused his death, but also about the role he had unwittingly played in her phobias during the nearly two decades since he had died. She told her uncle it was time to relieve him of this destructive position in her life. She asserted that with this memorial service, she was putting to rest the fears that had plagued her and replacing them with realistic information and memories about the life her uncle had lived. At the culmination of the ceremony, she dug a hole next to a tree and buried her uncle's cup, symbolically giving back to the earth the remains of her uncle's illness. Using a small gardener's shovel, she still needed her rubber gloves, but it was the first time she had ever voluntarily dug into "dirt."

The "relentless echoes" of her mother's fears became a central focus of the therapy, and several rituals were created to challenge and quiet them. One of the rituals consisted of a series of guided imagery journeys where Carla was, in her imagination, led to a pristine forest where a group of female elders befriended her and initiated her into the mysteries of living in harmony with nature. They were not timid about touching the earth and plant life, and she was progressively brought into pleasurable contact with trees, leaves, plants, and the ground from which they grew. The elders seemed very wise and capable of protecting her, and she began imagining that they were close by as she began to venture forth from her home without her "kit" in real life. In one guided imagery session, with the elders behind her lending their support, she confronted her mother, told her it was safe and beautiful to touch the earth, and, grabbing a handful of dirt, extended it to her mother as a gift. When her mother recoiled and refused the gift, Carla patiently explained to her that it was time for each of them to go forward on their own separate paths.

Another ritual in Carla's recovery involved clearing a "safe space" that did not require vigilant cleaning. She started with the wall next to her bed. She ceremonially cleared the wall and painted it a creamy white. On the wall she attached a feather her therapist had handed her after she had returned from one of her guided imagery sessions. She had studied it with fascination, forgetting for a moment that "I don't touch things like that!" She also posted on the wall a breathtaking color photo of an assemblage of plankton as seen through the microscope. She hung a prism next to the window so that it reflected rainbows over her bed and onto the wall. She imagined the rainbows as bridges that allowed the elders from the forest to send her support any time she was in need of protection. She designated this area as a sacred space that could not be defiled by obsessive cleaning. As the therapy progressed, this area was extended to include all four walls, then her entire bedroom, and eventually encompassed the entire home. While the impulse to clean was still strong in her, she made a realistic schedule of limits on the amount of time she would invest in cleaning and rewarded herself when she kept within that time. Gradually there was less need for the rigid schedule as she found other interests to be more compelling.

Toward the end of her counseling, Carla was encouraged to attend an art therapy class held in a ceramics studio. She was invited to represent the progress she had made through sculpture. It was exceedingly difficult for her to plunge her hands into the brown, sticky clay, but little by little she did. By the end of her therapy, she had made several pieces that were dipped in exotic glazes and ceremonially fired, losing their fragile, messy aspect and becoming lovely stone vessels. She put her "kit" into the kiln at the time of one of her last firings, transforming it to clean ash and smoke. The metaphor was deliberate. Of her fired pieces, one is a replica of a bar of soap, another is of her uncle's buried coffee mug, and a third is a much-worked figurine of one of her "elders."

The organic ritualistic elements of Carla's treatment reveal the essential connection between deep therapy and the individual's need for effective rites of passage. The following three cases demonstrate the use of psychologically sophisticated rituals outside of the therapy setting. These cases focus on creatively meeting the anguish of bereavement. One of the most important ways we can prepare to accept our own mortality is in the manner by which we come to terms with the deaths of those we love. The rituals illustrated in the following vignettes help the bereaved work through their grief, appreciate the love shared and the gifts gained from the one they have lost, and, in the face of death, reflect upon what truly matters in life.

CONTEMPORARY RITUALS FOR FACING LOSS

Imagine the distress as Christmas approaches shortly after the drowning of a family's infant son in their backyard swimming pool. The prospect of having to bear, amidst the surrounding revels of a festive holiday season, the unspeakable grief of having lost their freshest and dearest was anticipated with dread.

Faced with this dilemma, the Cortneys saw their choices as being either to take their three remaining children on a trip in an attempt to "skip" the holiday season altogether or to go ahead with their typical preparations and hope to somehow make it through a "business as usual" holiday. The therapist who was helping the family work through their bereavement, however, encouraged them to consider a third alternative, one that recognized that they were in a process of mourning, that mourning involves specific stages and tasks that may be embraced, and that they could use the holiday season to help them move onward in their grief process. They chose to make the holiday a very special "memorial Christmas" for Bobby. Although not an entirely joyous time, it was not entirely somber or at all hopeless. It was alive with authentic feelings, a deepening of bonds, and an honoring of a beloved bright child. The holiday turned out to be the essence of nondenial, a conscious, distinct commitment to healing.

The Cortneys identified three aspects of Christmas that focused the family's attention and could be used in honoring the memory of their son: gift giving, caroling, and decorating the tree. Throughout these activities, Bobby's picture was prominently displayed.

As the family exchanged gifts, each member, having had time in advance to think about what they would say, spoke of the gift Bobby had been in their lives. The impact of sharing gifts with one another was immeasurably deepened in an atmosphere that poignantly celebrated the preciousness of loved ones. Another family tradition for the Cortneys was to sing Christmas carols. That year they interspersed Bobby's favorite songs, "Itsy-Bitsy Spider" and "Muffin Man," with the traditional carols. To their surprise, they found that laughter broke through their tears, for some the first lightheartedness since Bobby's death. Finally, around the tree, they recalled fondly Bobby's first and only Christmas, when he intently observed the family members busily putting up the decorations and then proceeded to hang his own bent-handle spoon on a low branch. For every Christmas from then on, placing Bobby's spoon on the tree was an important part of the celebration.

As you saw with the Cortneys, the social potency of an established holiday can be an element that is worked into family rituals. For Brad and Myra East, dread of the coming Thanksgiving clouded their anticipations. Since their four children had grown and moved away, Thanksgiving was the holiday around which they all gathered in celebration. However, Myra's brother, Charlie, the family's favorite uncle, had died the previous June after a bout with lung cancer brought on by thirty-five years of smoking. Aunt Dee, widowed, depressed, and disoriented, was hard to be around and, from the time she'd married into the family, had never been anyone's favorite relative anyway.

In late October Myra, Brad, and the adult children discussed over the phone how they might use the upcoming Thanksgiving gathering to ritualize the loss of Uncle Charlie, whose presence had enlivened decades of Thanksgivings. Plans in place, Dee was gently informed that the holiday would be dedicated to Charlie's memory. She was asked to bring his favorite winter hat and other significant memorabilia with her. Despite her protests and trepidations, she was finally persuaded.

The theme of the day was "Thanks, God, for Charlie." Everyone spoke of favorite memories around the table. Later, with the men crashed in front of the television watching football, Charlie's cap sat on top of the set (where it was placed every successive Thanksgiving), keeping him ever present in spirit and sparking memories of his past enthusiasm.

At the end of the day, the Easts put Dee in the center of a hug circle and gave thanks for her (surprising themselves with their sincerity). Then they went to the backyard to ceremoniously plant a persimmon (Charlie's favorite fruit) tree. Under it they buried the old football he had always brought for them to toss around during half-time of the televised games. The fruit of that tree was ever after served as a Thanksgiving treat.

What might, without conscious choice and inventive ritual, have turned into a polite but forced holiday gathering became a memorable and deeply meaningful celebration of Charlie's life. Engineering such an outcome often requires courage as well as creativity. One of the bleakest holiday circumstances any of us is likely to face is widowhood in late middle age with children scattered and friends immersed in their own unbroken traditions. Loneliness, loss of purpose, and deep sorrow may lead to depression and even suicide.

Marge was sixty-seven when her husband died after thirty-eight years of marriage. Their two adult children were helpful in the beginning but soon returned to their active lives across the state. The first Christmas, Marge visited her daughter but felt alien and confused about her role. Worse, she feared she was a depressing, inconvenient element in their festivities, and whether or not this was accurate mattered less than her perception.

Resolved to do the next holiday season differently, Marge rose to the challenge of *re*-visioning her understanding of herself and the holiday season. Her role as the welcoming mother and matron to homecoming family was past. She didn't want to be a "tag-along" in her children's lives, and she began to cultivate a refreshed view of the possibilities.

Marge identified sources of her pleasure around the holidays, including food preparation, decorating, and gift giving. She resolved to keep what delighted her as she rethought the holiday experience.

Marge was a skilled watercolor artist, and she set about making small gifts and planning decorations with inventive themes and color combinations. Instead of the traditional turkey and mincemeat pie meal, she developed an original menu using elaborate Greek recipes.

Then, feeling excited, Marge contacted the local college for names of foreign students stranded in a strange country. She invited eight of them, and the party was a roaring success that became a delightful tradition and a source of important relationships for her throughout the year. By the second Christmas, she had twenty guests, all she could squeeze into her home.

Cultivating an Empowering Mythology for Confronting Death

Drawing upon the power of therapeutically informed ritual, *Mortal Acts* presents a series of structured experiences designed to usher you into fresh contact with your emotional core. In the process, your beliefs and attitudes about death, and the patterns of behavior that grow out of them, will be challenged. You might think of the personal rituals as internal "rites of passage," not from one stage of life to another but from one way of being with your mortality and into a more empowering relationship with it.

The rituals may be performed alone, with a friend, with family members, or as part of a small study group. Each ritual builds on those before it, so it is valuable to carry them out or at least read them in the order given.

Mortal Acts brings you into rugged emotional terrain. Please respect your own pace and needs. If after reading the instructions and case illustrations for a particular ritual you are reluctant to proceed with it, feel free to skip that ritual. Do, however, reflect on its purpose so you can bridge to the one that follows. The only materials you will need are a notebook or journal for describing and reflecting upon your experience with each ritual (some people use their personal computers), colored markers, a large paper plate, and optionally a cassette recorder with tapes. The personal rituals can be performed as you come to them in the text, or you can read the entire book and return to do them later. You may wish to go through some of the rituals more than one time. Use all you know about yourself to create the conditions that honor your style of learning and experiencing. For instance, a series of one-hour sittings or a concentrated weekend focusing on the program may be the better format for you.

Some people learn best through their eyes, others through their ears, others by movement. In designing these rituals we have, of necessity, chosen only a few of the possible ways to create the intended experiences. As you read through the instructions and the case examples, the intent of the ritual will become clear to you, and you can modify the suggestions to support your own natural learning style. For instance, many of the rituals involve "guided imagery" journeys. You may find that the guided imagery instructions work well for you, or you may find it more valuable to first read the instructions and then explore the suggested issues in your own manner, perhaps drawing your thoughts and feelings or expressing them in physical movement. Any of the instructions in this book can be adjusted to your own style and pace and taken spontaneously in unplanned directions.

If the imagery instructions, as they are presented, seem a good way for you to carry out the intent of the ritual, either have someone read them to you while you are deeply relaxed or read them yourself into a tape and then use the tape to guide you through the experience. A prerecorded tape of the guided imagery instructions, with meditative background music, is also available. (See the Supplemental Programs and Materials at the back of this book.)

Mortal Acts addresses some of the most profound and potentially instructive questions that can be asked. Take time to ready yourself. Sanctify the process by preparing a physical space that is peaceful and inspiring. Begin each ritual by mindfully bringing yourself into a state of deep relaxation. Meditate or simply calm your mind, and touch into the quiet before beginning your work with the ritual.

Steeped in the paradox that the inevitability of death can be a profound teacher, *Mortal Acts* offers step-by-step techniques for deeply affirming life. You will be examining your system of death denial, exploring ways of transcending death anxiety, and emerging from the process with a renewed and more inspiring personal mythology about death. The book closes with instruction for translating this renewed mythology about death into living more consciously and dynamically. From this journey through a profoundly challenging realm of your own interior, you will be learning how to draw upon an understanding of ritual to give you strength and inspiration in situations where terror, grief, and anger may seem raw and untamable.

GETTING STARTED:
Your Images About Death and Its Meaning

Preliminary to the program presented here for revising your mythology about death are three personal rituals to help you understand that mythology and explore its roots. In the first of these, you will be examining the beliefs and attitudes you now hold regarding death.

PERSONAL RITUAL 1: YOUR PHILOSOPHY OF DEATH

Articulating a "philosophy of death" can be a dynamic way to investigate your conscious outlook and values concerning the process of dying, the meaning of death, and the possibilities of afterlife. This first structured activity will focus on ideas and feelings that are readily accessible. The subsequent personal rituals will take you progressively deeper into an understanding of your unconscious beliefs and attitudes about these topics.

In beginning to verbalize your philosophy of death, you will be reflecting upon the positions you hold regarding some of death's mysteries. For instance, your deepest beliefs about afterlife—whether your life choices are oriented toward avoiding a fate of fire and brimstone, are focused on the material world with no concern about the hereafter, or are made within a secure sense of a better world to come—exert a subtle yet potent influence on the way you live.[1] Your philosophy of death will touch upon many other concerns as well, such as the way you have made sense of the deaths of those you have loved, the way you handle your own fears of death, and whatever meaning the fact that you will one day die adds to your life.

Put the heading "My Philosophy of Death" in your journal and place the following questions where you can glance at them easily. You will begin your "philosophy of death" statement by noting thoughts from your stream of consciousness as you reflect upon your beliefs, attitudes, and feelings about death. For at least ten uninterrupted minutes, write nonstop in your journal, producing an uncensored flow of thoughts and feelings in response to the following questions:

What is death?

Why do people die?

What happens when they die?

How do I feel about my own death?

It is not necessary to address all of the questions or to limit yourself to only these questions. The list is intended to stimulate your thoughts and feelings about death. An alternative approach is to speak for at least ten minutes, either to a person or into a tape recorder, ideas from your stream of consciousness about these questions and then to record a summary of your feelings and ideas in your journal.

Accompanying each of the personal rituals are descriptions of the experiences of two individuals as they went through the program. Their journal entries have been edited for clarity and brevity. The portions that are presented after each personal ritual demonstrate how that ritual may be carried out. You may want to read of their experiences with each ritual before you perform it. Peg Elliott Mayo served as a test subject while the program was being developed into its current form, and her journal work is presented. The second subject is Robert, a successful architectural engineer who had attended numerous self-development seminars and workshops over the previous decade. He was forty-four when he went through the program.

Once you have read Peg's and Robert's accounts, reflect on the four questions posed above and begin your stream of consciousness writing. When you have finished, further develop any of the thoughts. If you are having difficulty describing a particular feeling or dilemma, you might try to capture it with another form of expression, such as drawing or movement.

When you have completed your stream of consciousness state-ment, there is an optional next step. Rework these initial reflections into a more coherent "philosophy of death" statement. Organize the spontaneous writing into a meaningful essay. Finally, whether you stopped with your original thoughts or proceeded to rewrite them, underline the most important or most troubling ideas you have expressed. You will be using these underlined phrases in the fol-lowing personal ritual.

From Peg's Philosophy of Death

"Death closes the circle. It means immobility. Coldness. Stillness. Peace. Silence. <u>Gone.</u> Missing. Dissolving. Nonbeing. A doorway to another consciousness. Loss of self. Loss of body. <u>Loss.</u> Unknown. Forgetfulness. Being forgotten. Loss of control. Loss of influence. Giving up all that is familiar. Being stripped of all that is known. Theoretically, it is all right, even good. Gutwise, it is frightening.

"People die to make room for more people. To escape intolera-ble conditions. To fertilize the lilies. To make compost. Because their lessons are learned. Because they refuse to learn their lessons. Because their lessons are incomprehensible. Because other people don't cher-ish them. For hopelessness. For loneliness. For love. For fatigue. Because it's time. Because God 'calls them home.' Because we are biological entities with a limited potential for self-repair and an in-tolerance for pain. <u>Because we are cyclical/seasonal and there is no holding back time.</u>

"How do I feel about my own death? Rude question. On one level I want to control it. I had no conscious choice about life. Seems only fair. Suicide is always a possibility, an inevitable part of my au-tonomy and self-determination. What other authority is there? I wouldn't do it spitefully, out of anger or immediate panic. That's a promise. I wouldn't do it ugly. But I reserve the right to do it. <u>I fear pain, dependency, ugliness, and loss of control. Pity from others. Being tolerated. Doctors with tubes and shots and knives and drugs.</u> I want my dignity! I don't want to crap my bed as my last act and be remembered wasted and helpless. I don't trust others to let me die in good season; I'm afraid they'll keep me alive as a semblance out of misguided love or duty. Spare me duty.

"On another level, I want to avoid death at all costs. No matter how long I live, it won't be long enough to learn all the crafts I want, take all the river walks I love, laugh with my friends, write stories, eat ripe persimmons, caress my man, play with my dog, live! What could be better than this world? I can see stars and anemones, taste spring water and hot chocolate, hear the river's song and my husband's laugh, touch alder bark and a grandchild's round head, smell musky humus in the forest and a man's sweat after splitting wood. I am alive in my senses: I can dance and weep, hunger and stretch, learn and do. What do I think of my own death? That it is premature, whenever it happens. I've been a laggard scholar: too many lessons of appreciation, patience, generosity, honor, mercy, humility left to learn. I need more time. I need more time.

"Something is eluding me. I'm somehow not coming to grips with the questions. Let's boil it down. I'm terrified to *die*—something in me is *terrified* of how I'll behave during the process. Will I wipe out all good memories in the minds of those who know me to the end? Will I snivel? Or scream? Will I be a toothless hag? Who will wipe my ass? Do I have to learn this hideous lesson? Please, please no! Can't I avoid it? I don't trust my strength not to be disgusting.

"I'm worried about the process of dying—but death itself is not frightening in the same way. It is almost intriguing, like a journey to a foreign place that I've studied a good deal. I feel better when I tell myself hopeful, visionary stories about what will be. Maybe I will have a nice passing—something natural. Get weak, want to rest, feel a 'rightness' in dying. I don't know. I hope so."

From Robert's Philosophy of Death

"I don't usually experience a fear of death, but I get very frightened at the thought of something taking me prematurely. The fear is most strongly focused on my fear of things that would rip up my body. That's a thought that really terrifies me. I have visions of something crushing my head, of a knife going into my belly, of unbeatable pain and the terrible moment of realizing I'm about to be forcefully yanked out of this world—no preparation, no good-byes. An instant death would not be my choice as compared with the thought of dying of ripe old age, but if the other choice were seeing my body getting wracked up, feeling the pain, dealing with the horror, I'd rather have it be instant. Lights out.

"I never think of myself as being afraid of death—my spiritual beliefs give me comfort on that score—but I guess the fear of getting physically mangled masks any other fear of death that may be there. I feel that fear every time I read newspaper and magazine stories about others' tragedies, and I have my share of nightmarish daydreams as well. Perhaps I also have fears of death that I keep out of my mind just because death seems so far off in the future that it isn't a looming concern. So maybe if I do have some underlying fear of death, I just never allow it to surface. Maybe death is too far off to be a concern right now. Or if death is going to come sooner, it will take such violence to cut me off from life at this point that my focus is on the gore involved in dying instead of the fact of death.

"But I also think I'm not consciously afraid of death because I find peace in my belief that living here in the world is the hardest part of existence—that on the other side it's all about love and peace. I think of life as a great experiment in which the realm of spirit is trying to manifest itself in this denser physical world, where spirit takes on flesh and sensation. I think of death not as an end but as a change of scenery, a new stage and form for the spirit in an eternally evolving drama. And a blissful one. That vision offers comfort!

"But what if it isn't all that black and white—harsh here, glorious there? Nothing else seems to be. I don't like thoughts that upset my notion of death as a continuation of conscious being in perfect peace and harmony. I guess I could accept something in-between, but I feel myself wanting to bargain for a vision of death that isn't too bad. I can certainly think of much scarier versions of death than anything I want to consider. I'm not sure where my faith comes that the nicer vision is the truer one, but everything in me wants to hang onto it."

PERSONAL RITUAL 2: EXPLORATION OF A
PERSONAL CONCERN ABOUT DEATH

Reread the phrases you underlined in your "philosophy of death" statement. Choose the one that evokes the strongest unsettling feeling in you or the one that you would most like to explore. Peg chose "I need more time." Robert considered choosing the statement "I don't like thoughts that upset my notion of death as a continuation of conscious being in perfect peace and harmony." But the concern seemed somewhat remote to him. The statement he finally selected was "seeing my body getting wracked up."

In carrying out these guided imagery instructions, it is important to realize that many people do not actually *see* clear pictures in their minds. They may know what they know through what they call intuition, by hearing an inner narration, by seeing abstract images, or by directly sensing the thought or memory. Thinking usually involves some combination of these modes, and when we use the terms *visualization* and *imagery,* we are referring to the blend that occurs within you.

We will also remind you that in this and each subsequent personal ritual that uses guided imagery, you will need to decide which method you will use for leading yourself through the experience (reading the instructions into a tape, asking someone to read them to you, using the prerecorded tape, or becoming familiar enough with the instructions that you can create an experience that accomplishes the intent of the ritual). Robert used the prerecorded tape that led him through the guided imagery instructions; Peg, after reading the text until she understood the essence of each ritual, innovated a personalized version of it. She would think about the question raised, meditate, and set time aside to create an inner experience based on the idea of the ritual.

If you tape the instructions or have someone read them to you, they should be read slowly and deliberately. Pause for about ten seconds each time you come to the word *pause* and each time you come to the end of a paragraph. At any point during a guided visualization where you need more time to allow a particular image to develop or to carry out an instruction, simply signal to your partner or turn off the tape. After reviewing the statement from your "philosophy of death" that you would like to explore further, find a comfortable position, close your eyes, and begin to relax.

As you settle into this safe, secure spot, focus on your breathing. Release any tension in your body. [Pause.] Listen for and feel each in breath and each out breath. [Pause.] Notice how your stomach and chest fill . . . and empty. [Pause.] As you continue to breathe and relax, you are better able to concentrate on my voice and on the suggestions I will offer. If outside sounds or passing thoughts cross your mind, they fade quietly into the background just as they occur, like autumn leaves being carried away by the wind. Your breathing is slow and deep as you relax more completely with each of your next five breaths. One [pause]; two [pause]; three [pause]; four [pause]; five [pause].

Bring to mind the key statement you chose from your "philosophy of death." [Pause.] Notice the feelings evoked in you as you recall this thought. [Pause.] Focus on the part of your body in which these feelings are the strongest. [Pause.] Bring your attention to this part of your body. [Pause.] Experience this part of your body through your breathing, your muscles, and your inner imagery. [Pause.] Find a word or a phrase that describes the way this part of your body feels.

In a moment, you will imagine yourself expressing this feeling in some new ways. First you will see yourself expressing the feeling through movement. If you were to dance this feeling, how would you dance? [Pause.]

Imagine yourself expressing your feeling through movement. [Pause.] Do your movements seem free or constricted? [Pause.] Does your dance accurately portray the feeling it is expressing? [Pause.] Continue the dance in your mind and let it evolve. [20-second pause.]

Allow the dance to come to a close now, and imagine yourself settling into a relaxed, centered, calm position. [Pause.] You are about to create a clay sculpture of your feeling. Imagine that you are holding soft clay. You begin to work the clay with your hands. You are creating a sculpture that represents your feeling. Your sculpture may look like something that you recognize, or it may be abstract. [Pause.] Soon, your sculpture is complete. [Pause.] Experience it with your eyes and hands. [Pause.] Has its color changed from that of the original clay? [Pause.] How does it feel in your hands? [Pause.] What does it show you about your original feelings? [Pause.] Get to know this sculpture. [Pause.] If your sculpture could come to life and speak to you, what would it say? [Pause.] In the following pause, sense what it has to tell you about the underlined phrase from your "philosophy of death." [60-second pause.]

It is nearly time now to come back to your normal waking consciousness. You can slowly begin to return to the present moment. Counting from five back to one, you will be able to recall all you need of this experience. When you hear the number one, you will feel alert, relaxed, and refreshed, as if returning from a wonderful nap. Five, moving your fingers and your toes. [Pause.] Four, stretching your shoulders, neck, and face muscles. [Pause.] Three, taking a deep breath. [Pause.] Two, bringing your attention back into the room. [Pause.] And one, opening your eyes, feeling refreshed, confident, and able to effectively and creatively meet the requirements of your day.

Summarize this experience in your journal by reflecting on the following questions. On which thought from your "philosophy of death" did you focus? What feeling did it evoke in you? How did you experience that feeling in your body? How did you express that feeling in movement? What did the sculpture look like? What did the sculpture have to tell you?

Peg's Summary

Starting with her statement "I need more time," Peg identified her most prominent feeling as an eagerness to get on with her life. "It centers on my face, which is the locus of my senses (eyes, ears, nose, mouth, skin). My dance is a wild one, around a blazing campfire on the banks of the river. I am fluid, uninhibited, and firelike in my movements. The light reflects on the water with great beauty. I form a flowing, abstract shape with the clay—it has the appearance of a flame. It doesn't speak to me, but there is a 'knowingness' that seems part mind, part intuition that says this flame is primal, that its existence is dependent on fuel and oxygen (as mine is), and that it is without morality, sentiment, or thought—it simply *is.* That for it to do work, do harm, or be controlled takes a sort of intelligence that is not implicit to the fire. Same as me. The burning flame represents an inevitability about life and, therefore, about death. Even my very important death. *I need more time.* I will live with the gusto of a campfire, but I know—eager or not, reluctant or nor—when the fuel is gone, so am I."

Robert's Summary

"I started by focusing on my fear of a violent death. In my body, I could feel a tenseness in my throat and a hardness in my stomach when I thought of dying that way. As I imagined dancing the tenseness, I only saw myself crouching up in a fetal position with my hands protecting my head. I didn't make a sculpture, because my little crouched version of myself just became the sculpture. When it could talk with me, it said, 'You are much more afraid of death than you know, and the fear has something to teach you. First, while much is out of your control regarding the dreadful things that could happen to you, there is also much you can do to prevent or not invite such things. Still, no matter what you do, tragic possibilities remain. But that is the lot of all of humanity.' Then the little sculpture scolded me for not taking greater enjoyment in the life I have. 'If there is anything the threat of sudden loss ought to teach you,' he said, 'it is that the failure to savor the life you are living is a loss of the greatest magnitude.' His words hit hard. They cause me to think."

PERSONAL RITUAL 3: CREATION OF YOUR DEATH SHIELD

Native American cultures often used sacred shields for prayer, purification, and healing ceremonies. An image received in a powerful dream or during a vision quest might be interpreted by the tribal shaman, painted on a circular hide, and adorned with feathers, fur, tassels, or shells. The symbols on the shield might tell of the person's history, ritual identity, or aspirations. The shield offered guidance and spiritual protection. We would like you to think of the death shield you are about to construct as an ally as you go through this program, there to help you face your fears of death and to access a sense of the sacred in your daily life.

Your death shield should be about a foot in diameter. You should be able to draw or paint on it. Some people have created their death shields out of rawhide stretched over a rim made of willow. Others have made a shield by putting unbleached muslin in an embroidery hoop and using textile paints. Simpler methods are to use the back of a large paper plate or to cut a piece of white construction paper into a circle. You will need crayons, colored markers, or a paint palette.

Draw a line through the center of your shield, dividing it in half. Draw a second line so that your shield is divided like a pie cut into four equal pieces. On the outer rim, label each section with one of the following phrases: "First Memories About Death," "Death Fears," "Transcending Death Anxiety," and "A Renewed Mythology About Death." Once you have constructed your death shield, use the following instructions to evoke the imagery that you will draw onto the section labeled "First Memories About Death." Later, you will be drawing images on the other three sections of your shield to symbolize your experiences as you perform subsequent personal rituals. When you have completed your death shield, it will serve as a succinct overview of your work in this program.

In the following guided imagery journey, you will be taken back in your memory and helped to find a symbol that you will draw on this first section of your shield. When people mentally return to earlier times in their lives, they may not be sure if their memories are accurate. Know that any images that arise, even if totally from your imagination, are a reflection of your inner life in response to the ritual, and will serve the purposes here.

Make the preparations for another guided visualization experience. Tape-record the instructions, arrange to have someone read them to you, or familiarize yourself with them well enough so you can create an experience that accomplishes the intent of the ritual. Look at the section of your death shield labeled "First Memories About Death." With your journal, shield, and drawing implements nearby, find a comfortable position, close your eyes, and begin to relax.

As you settle into this safe, secure spot, focus on your breathing. Release any tension in your body. [Pause.] Listen for and feel each in breath and each out breath. [Pause.] Notice how your stomach and chest fill . . . and empty. [Pause.] As you continue to breathe and relax, you are better able to concentrate on my voice and on the suggestions I will offer. If outside sounds or passing thoughts cross your mind, they fade quietly into the background just as they occur. Your breathing is slow and deep as you relax more completely with each of your next five breaths. One [pause]; two [pause]; three [pause]; four [pause]; five [pause].

You are about to come to a memory from early in your life. You will slide backward in time, safely and securely allowing yourself to recall the sensation of being very young and naive. You will come upon a scene from your past that involved one of your earliest encounters with the reality of death. Perhaps you saw something in a movie or on television that brought this awareness to you. It might have been the death of a pet, a neighbor, a relative, or a friend. [Pause.] If more than one memory comes to you, select one you would like to examine in greater detail.

Breathing deeply now, feel yourself, with your next three breaths, going back to this earlier scene. One, know that you are well protected. Two, smoothly and surely, you are moving back in time toward the earlier scene. Three, you are in the scene, and you begin to survey it.

You can see yourself more clearly now. You understand your feelings and have great insight into their basis. Recall the details—place, time, circumstances. [Pause.] Notice who is with you. [Pause.] Sense what they are feeling. [Pause.] How did they involve you? [Pause.] Did they offer comfort? [Pause.] Observe how the attitudes held by your parents or other adults were conveyed to you. [Pause.] Recognize the attitudes you came to hold regarding death. [Pause.] Spend a few more moments examining this scene. [20-second pause.]

Focus on a sensation in your body that relates to this experience. Identify the part of your body where this sensation is the most intense. [Pause.] Find the shape of the sensation—notice its borders. [Pause.] See its color. [Pause.] Explore its texture. [Pause.] In a moment, you will recognize a symbol emerging out of these shapes and colors.

Watch as a symbol that you associate with this earlier experience appears. [Pause.] You may actually see the symbol take form, or you may simply sense what it is. It will further evolve over the next few moments. Relax as it becomes increasingly clear. [20-second pause.]

As a fitting symbol emerges from your memory, prepare to draw it on your shield. [Pause.] Return to the present moment and take several deep breaths. [Pause.] Begin to stretch your body. [20-second pause.] Gently open your eyes and draw the symbol on the portion of your shield labeled "First Memories About Death." As you draw the symbol, you may find that it is changing even as you are creating it or that you have more than one image to draw. Draw whatever comes. Do not be concerned about what may be "aesthetic" or "correct." As long as the drawing is meaningful to you, it will serve its purpose. When you have completed

*your drawing, you will find that you have returned to full waking con-
sciousness, feeling refreshed, confident, and able to effectively and creatively meet the requirements of your day.*

If you wish, you may examine other scenes as well. Return to the
paragraph that begins "You are about to come to a memory from
early in your life." Carry out the instructions from there. You may repeat this sequence one or more times. When you have completed the
"First Memories" portion of your death shield to your satisfaction,
consciously breathe out and physically shake out any unpleasant sensations in your body.

In your journal, under a heading called "My First Memories
About Death," describe your experiences with this exercise. Focus
particularly on the attitudes you came to hold regarding death as a result of this experience.

Finally, experiment with a technique that we call "creative projection." In this technique, you project yourself into a symbol you want
to further investigate, identifying with it as if you *are* that symbol. In
your imagination, you "become" the symbol. Try this with the symbol (or one of the symbols) drawn on the first portion of your death
shield. Imagine yourself as that symbol. Begin to describe yourself as
the symbol, staying in the present tense, active voice: "I am a . . . " If
the symbol on your shield were a whale, you might begin, "I am a big,
blue whale. I can disappear under the water for a long, long time,
but I always come up again. Sometimes when I go under the water it
seems . . . " Continue to write, or speak into a tape or to a partner,
for several minutes while "staying in character" and allowing a story to
develop as you describe—in the voice of your symbol—yourself, your
needs, and your purpose for being. Finally, reflect in your journal
upon any further understanding of the symbol's significance.

Peg's Early Memory and First Death Shield Symbol

"I was four when my Grandma Lampkin died. My Irish grand-
mother. With the brogue and the lemon meringue pie. I didn't

know about dying or that she was sick. She was eighty-seven, but that meant nothing. They told me she'd 'gone to heaven.' I wanted to go with her, and I was mad she'd gone without telling me. I thought going to heaven was like going to town or someplace 'real.' Everyone crying made me cry. I can remember them telling me she was 'happy now' (I never thought of her as anything else) and that I could see her 'someday.' It was then I got really upset—I knew I needed more time with her *now;* I felt something important was missing, and I still do.

"What I learned was that I was excluded from the important parts of dying and that there were a lot of promises that didn't comfort my loss. I learned death was for grown-ups to deal with, but that since it was 'just like going to sleep' it could happen to anyone at any time. Even little me.

"An image of Grandma Lampkin's brass bed with the red-and-white quilt she'd made to cover it came to me. I saw the huge down pillows, their lace-edged cases embroidered with strawberries and violets. There was the smell of lavender. The bed is empty. Neat. Cold. I'm never again going to climb in with her, cuddle up, feel her soft breasts under the flannel nightie against my back. I'm never again going to hear, in that lilting whisper in the dark, stories of 'the Faery' or what the trip to America was like. Never. Never. Never.

"I feel very young and abandoned. I can remember no psychic pain that precedes this memory. I realize that 'young and abandoned' is the root of my feelings about bereavement. I feel vulnerable regarding my own death. I question, 'Where did she go?' and, more urgently, 'Why did she go? Was I bad? Is she mad at me? Is that why she went? Will she come back if I am very, very good? What if Daddy dies? What will happen to me? *What will happen to me?*'

"The beautiful empty bed is my death shield symbol. 'I am a big brass bed. I'm a place for cuddles and stories. I'm safe and warm. People have made love—made babies—in me. I've heard the whispers in the dark. I'm a place for touching and resting. I'm strong, and

I've been around a long time. My mattress has a hollow where two people have lain, spoon style, for many the long hour. Sometimes it was the man and woman, other times the woman and children. I'm marked with menstrual blood and the blood of giving birth. There are transparent yellow rings of spent semen. I have a stain from spilled tea, taken by a sick child seeking comfort. And no one uses me anymore. I'm some sort of shrine. Everything is too neat. My pillowcases don't show the dent of resting heads; no bodies mound up my linen sheets and bright quilt. People look at me and sigh or weep. They remember me as I was for them and never notice that I could still be used. I am very sad.' "

Robert's Early Memory and First Death Shield Symbol

"I was about twelve. My parents went to a play with friends. One of them had a heart attack and died. I had never seen my mother cry before. This was not something adults did. I saw her struggle not to cry. I saw her cry. I didn't know what to do. We never talked about the death. My questions evoked discomfort, and I quickly dropped the subject. But I learned that my mother thought death was too terrible to talk about. I learned it was something that even the great and wise world of adults could not control. And I learned that it made you have awful emotions that you also could not control.

"I drew a face on my death shield. It was a face because I didn't know how to draw a scream. When I remembered the scene with my mother, I felt she needed more than the few tears that fought their way through. She needed to scream. I felt in my body how unable she was to express the depths of her feelings. And I felt in my body how unable I became to scream my screams and cry my tears. So on my shield I drew a face that was screaming. It was my mother's scream, the scream she never screamed for the death of her friend. Okay, 'I am the face that needs to scream. I am tense. I'm in agony, so I shut off my feelings. All my feelings. I'm very sad, though I feel only my deadness. I need to scream. I must scream. A scream starts from my belly, rises in my throat, and escapes as a haunting wail.'

"Having this unuttered scream make itself heard some thirty years hence releases something in me. It opens my inhibitions, opens my flow of energy, opens my ability to embrace life in both its horrors and its joys."

THE FIRST STAGE:
Rattling Your System of Death Denial

Beneath the level of daily activity, beneath the level of our un-spoken beliefs, lies the raw, primal, undiluted terror of death. We know this terror with the approaching sound of skidding tires on a slick roadway, the abrupt appearance of an ominous figure on a dark street, or the surreal perils of a nightmare. The terror is a reflex, an in-born response, so that a threat to our survival instantly mobilizes us for action. No other order of business even begins to compete. As Samuel Johnson once put it, "When a man knows he is to be hanged in a fortnight, it concentrates his mind wonderfully."

The terror that arises when we believe our lives are in danger, even if it is a fleeting terror, usually leaves a lingering impression. When we were children, we were particularly vulnerable to becoming en-snared in a tangle of overwhelming fears, and we generally gave such experiences a prominent spot in our evolving cosmologies. As Ernest Becker describes it, children have

> their recurrent nightmares, their universal phobias of insects and mean dogs. In their tortured interiors radiate complex symbols of many inadmissible realities—terror of the world, the horror of one's own wishes, the fear of vengeance by the parents, the disappearance of things, one's lack of control over anything, really. It is too much for any animal to take, but the child has to take it, and so he wakes up screaming with almost punctual regularity during the period where his weak ego is in the process of consolidating things.[1]

The child's first primitive attempts at this lifelong "process of con-solidating things" establish the foundations of an evolving mythology about death. Irvin Yalom describes the stages by which the child comes to terms with being mortal.[2] Although the parents' explanations and the feelings they model give some structure to the toddler's emerging awareness of death, they hardly provide adequate comfort for the primary anxiety that grows out of this awareness. Gradually, with the budding psychological defenses of preadolescence, the child develops "efficient and sophisticated forms of denial, awareness glides into the unconscious," and the overwhelming fear of death is contained. But the awareness of fear will break through again: "During adolescence, childhood denial systems are no longer effective. The introspective tendencies and the greater resources of the adolescent permit him or her to face, once again, the inevitability of death, to bear the anxiety, and to search for an alternate mode of coping with the facts of life."[3]

Psychological defense mechanisms such as repression, displacement, rationalization, and "personal efforts to overcome death through a wide variety of strategies that aim at achieving symbolic immortality"[4] allow us to emotionally manage the fear of death. Some of these defenses may lead to highly constructive activities; others may involve a broad array of foolish pursuits. Ernest Becker's book *The Denial of Death*[5] persuasively argues that the fear of death is a core motivating factor in the wanton accumulation of wealth, fame, and power (parodied in the bumper sticker "He who dies with the most toys wins"). Successful coping with life requires that effective means be found for coming to terms with the inevitability of death. Inadequate attempts to transcend the fear of dying have, in fact, been directly linked to psychopathology.[6]

Later, in the second stage of the program, you will examine ways of coping with the underlying fear of death, and you will explore the most constructive approaches you can envision for transcending that fear. In this first stage, however, the focus is on the fear of death itself.

In advising psychotherapists to uncover their clients' repressed anxieties about death, Yalom emphasizes that this is not a call to a morbid preoccupation with death but rather a reminder that when one is able to become more conscious about the nature of being, including the certainty of death, life becomes richer. He quotes Santayana: "The dark background which death supplies brings out the tender colors of life in all their purity."[7] He also points out that the therapist does not have to create the experience of death anxiety but rather help the person recognize what is already there: "Ordinarily we deny, or selectively attend to, reminders of our existential situation; the task of the therapist is to reverse the process, to pursue these reminders, for they are not enemies but powerful allies in the pursuit of integration and maturity."[8] The following three personal rituals are tools to help you gently tap into your own anxieties regarding death, recognized and repressed, and to place them into a meaningful framework.

PERSONAL RITUAL 4: OPENING YOUR HEART TO YOUR DEEPER FEARS

This fourth personal ritual calls upon you to arrange a visit with someone who is in the midst of confronting his or her own mortality. While requiring some effort and courage, the exercise can lead to a valuable encounter. The person can be an acquaintance or someone you have never met. If no one comes to mind, your local hospice may be willing to arrange such a meeting, or if you go to a nursing home, the staff will probably be happy to introduce you to someone whose faculties are intact and who is eager to talk. Sensitive human contact from outside the institution is a scarce and precious resource for many people in such settings. If it would provide a useful structure for your visit, or simply make you more comfortable, you may accurately represent the visit as part of an educational program that suggests you expose yourself to individuals who may be in the final stages of life.

Prepare for your visit by cultivating your curiosity about what it is like for this person who is approaching death. Begin by stating that you are there to learn how life appears from the vantage point of one who is further along the path than you. What made life most meaningful? Are there regrets? How does the future appear? Engage in conversation that encourages discussion about whatever the person feels is important. Particularly open your heart to the fears or frustrations she or he may be experiencing. With sensitivity and utmost respect for the person's dignity, follow your curiosity. Listen with compassion and deepen the conversation by conveying your interest. If the person brings up the topic of death, do not be afraid to pursue it, but do not push your way into sensitive areas he or she seems to be avoiding. Your only job is to be a good listener. You are not trying to influence the person's attitudes or beliefs in any way. Listen, observe, and learn. Notice in particular the feelings the discussion generates in you.

If this assignment seems too uncomfortable or time consuming and you decide against carrying it out, at least set aside half an hour and role-play a conversation between yourself and the person you imagine you might have found through a hospice or at a nursing home. Assume both of the roles described above. With two chairs facing one another, literally switch positions as you go from being yourself to being the other person. If you yourself are in the final season of your life, place in the other chair a naive interviewer, someone who is puzzled about feelings of impending death and wants to understand your experience. Continue the dialogue until you have reached a satisfactory depth.

In your journal, record your experience and your feelings. Focus particularly on this question: In what ways was this visit and interview [whether it was an actual or a role-played visit] a catalyst that opened me to fears about death that are usually outside my awareness?

Fears Touched by Peg's Visit

"Being old and abandoned. Weak. Confused. Subject to. Dependent. Unloved. Wasted. All the years wasted. But my fears are about dying, not death. Death, if I were Hilda [the woman she visited], would be water in the desert. It's living sick and old that seems grotesque, intolerable, a humiliation. The dying part. She has pain, and they give her pills and a pat on the head. No one holds her. No one meets her questioning eyes. No one comes to see her, but she has an institutional aluminum Christmas tree on her windowsill. She remembers snow on Christmas, 'up to your belly.' She knows she's outlived her usefulness. She knows it's time to go, but *they won't let her.* The IV unit runs four hours every day, and the hiss of oxygen never stops. She can't leave her bed except as a burden to someone stronger. She sits on a sheepskin to keep down the bedsores. And this woman used to dig field lilies for a living. She raised seven children; she lived through the Depression and was a World War II widow. She was capable and tough. Now look at her."

Fears Touched by Robert's Visit

"I visited John Parnelli [a neighbor who was dying of cancer]. He's going to leave the boys and Johanna behind him. He is mad and miserable. He can't quite believe it's happening. Neither can I. I certainly can't understand why. He is so young. Here death seems senseless and cruel. It tries my faith that justice has anything to do with the Big Plan. When I put myself in John's place, I can feel a lot of fear. Besides the unthinkable losses—delightful wife, wonderful kids, promising future—and the pain, there is that impending date to go over the edge and into the unknown. The prospect seems chillingly unpredictable and desperately lonely."

PERSONAL RITUAL 5: THE FEAR OF DEATH AT ITS FOUNDATION

Head a new page of your journal "My Fears About Death." Review your experiences with the first four personal rituals. Remain particularly alert for areas where fear is evident. Describe these in your journal. Were some of these fears previously outside your awareness?

What are the effects of first recognizing them? Take the time to consider these questions carefully in your journal. Among the fears Peg identified were those of "pain, dependency, ugliness, and loss of control. Pity from others. Being tolerated. Doctors with tubes and shots and knives and drugs." Robert focused on the feeling he attributed to his neighbor, that death seemed "chillingly unpredictable and desperately lonely."

When you have written as much as you have to say, reread your words. With your death shield and colored markers nearby, find a comfortable position, close your eyes, and begin to relax.

As you settle into this safe, secure spot, focus on your breathing. Release any tension in your body. [Pause.] Listen for and feel each in breath and out breath. [Pause.] Notice how your stomach and chest fill . . . and empty. [Pause.] As you continue to breathe and relax, you are better able to concentrate on my voice and on the suggestions I will offer. If outside sounds or passing thoughts cross your mind, they fade quietly into the background just as they occur. Your breathing is slow and deep as you relax more completely with each of your next five breaths. One [pause]; two [pause]; three [pause]; four [pause]; five [pause].

You have been giving much thought to your fear of death. [Pause.] The fear of death is not new to you. When you were a child, you had many fears about death. You may remember the terror of a nightmare or of a monster that you imagined had crawled under your bed or into your closet. You may have feared for your own life or the life of a parent or other loved one. You are about to focus on one of these fears from your childhood. You may return to the same experience you identified in one of the previous personal rituals or to a different one. Pull yourself back to being very young and feeling your fear. [Pause.] Feel yourself moving back in time now to this early experience of your fear of death. [Pause.] Where are you? What is occurring? Who is there? [30-second pause.]

You are about to find a symbol of these fears. Focus on a sensation in your body that relates to this early experience. Identify the part of your body where this sensation is the most intense. [Pause.] Find the shape of the sensation—notice its borders. [Pause.] See its color. [Pause.] Explore its texture. [Pause.] In a moment, you will recognize a symbol emerging out of these shapes and colors.

Watch as the symbol appears. [Pause.] You may actually see the symbol take form, or you may simply sense what it is. It will further evolve over the next few moments. Relax as it becomes increasingly clear. [20-second pause.] This symbol represents your fear of death, and you will be able to remember it so you can, in a little while, draw it on your shield.

First bring your attention back to your early experience. Again, see yourself as a child who knows the fear of death. [Pause.] Now imagine an adult entering the scene. The adult is you at your current age. You have traveled back in time to give support to this young, frightened child. As an adult, you are not afraid of the fear and vulnerability you see in the child. You may even feel touched by the child's innocence. From your compassion for this child, you are able to provide the comfort or affection that you sincerely needed when you were young and frightened. Imagine yourself providing that comfort and affection now. [30-second pause.] In addition to comfort and affection, you have some advice and information about the path that lies ahead. Allow a conversation to develop between your current self and this younger self. Hear the words, see the expressions, feel the contact. [60-second pause.]

Now gently place your adult hands upon the child and lovingly communicate peaceful, curative energies to the small body. Your hands are able to bring about a healing of old emotional wounds left over from this period of your life. [30-second pause.]

It is time to say good-bye for now to this inner child. Allow yourself to embrace this young person. [Pause.] Take a few last moments together and then say a heartfelt good-bye. [20-second pause.]

Again recall the symbol representing your fear of death. Does it feel different now? Prepare to draw this symbol on your shield. [Pause.] Take several deep breaths and begin to stretch your body. [20-second pause.] Open your eyes and draw the symbol on the portion of your shield that is labeled "Death Fears." As you draw this symbol, you may find that it is changing even as you are creating it or that you have more than one image to draw. Draw whatever comes. When you have completed your drawing, you will find that you have returned to full waking consciousness, feeling refreshed, confident, and able to effectively and creatively meet the requirements of your day.

In your journal, describe the scene you remembered and what occurred when you went back there as an adult. Also, reflect on the meaning of the symbol or symbols you drew on your shield. Consider using the creative projection technique for further examining its personal significance, "becoming" the symbol as you did earlier and describing yourself as that symbol, using first-person present tense.

Peg's Journey Back in Time and Her Death Fear Symbol

"Throughout my childhood, my mother was very sick. She spent much of her time at home in a hospital bed. I can vividly remember, every few weeks, overhearing as she told my father, in terror, that she was about to die. When I went back in time, I told the little girl that it means her mother is afraid and in pain. I was as eloquent as I know how in making the point that she was not to connect the misery she witnessed in her mother with her own being. As a child, I made such a powerful commitment to be just the opposite of my mother that it has influenced my character in major dysfunctional ways. I addressed this in my visit back in time. I was one adult in her young life who rewarded her with more than words reinforcing her stoicism. I showed her how to pick and choose her responses. Most of all, I loved her and accepted her for who she was.

"My death shield symbol is a hospital bed with lots of equipment on it. 'I am a hospital bed. I've held a lot of pain and terror. I'm a place to suffer and die. I can keep your lungs working with my oxygen pumps. I can fill you with saline and glucose solutions and keep your electrolytes in balance. I have catheters to empty your bladder into a yellow bag, and I have oversized diapers for you to wear. I have a button you can push, and sooner or later someone will come to roll you over or wipe the slobber off your chin. I can support your every function from breathing to digesting to moving, but I'm a place to die, not live. I am very, very threatening.' "

Robert's Journey Back in Time and His Death Fear Symbol

"I went back to a nightmare I had when I was very young. I'm not sure if it was a memory or just my imagination, but it felt real enough. I was gripped by an immobilizing terror. I wanted to scream, but I couldn't. I could barely open my mouth. It wasn't that I was inhibited the way my mother seemed to be in the other exercise—I was frozen.

"The picture that emerged from the cold sensations in my chest was, at first, a big cube of ice. Then it became a heart. It was my heart. Frozen. Cold. Scared. I remembered the word *chilling* from my experience with John Parnelli.

"When the adult me went back to find the child, the child's chest and heart were frozen. Out of fear, it seemed. I placed my hands over the heart. The heart started to thaw. The child started to scream and cry. I just held him and provided understanding and comfort. Being able to scream, cry, and be understood made the whole predicament a little less terrifying. Nothing needed to be said. Perhaps that thawing of the child's heart also helps to thaw this adult's heart of a coldness that goes all the way back to once having closed down against horrendous, unnamed terrors?"

PERSONAL RITUAL 6: CREATION OF A DEATH FABLE, "DEATH IN THE SHADOW OF FEAR"

In your journal or speaking into a tape recorder, write a death fable. Death fables share common themes. They depict a poignant scene of a person who is dying; they speak to the particular and to the universal, to the conscious and the unconscious; they are not bound by ordinary rules of logic; and they are often typified by extremes (the main character may be very, very rich or very, very poor, kind or cruel, simple or wise). You may set your story in any particular period of history, in a tribal culture, within a family of animals or elves, or in any other context you wish. In your death fable, the main character is dying and knows it. Moreover, this character happens to have the same fears about death that you have identified. All other details are up to you. Your character may be male or female, young or old, and about to die from any cause.

Once you have read Peg's and Robert's death fables, center yourself, relax in a comfortable spot with your journal nearby, and contemplate the death fable you are about to create. Allow your story to emerge from deep within you. Set the scene and fully describe how the person first learns that death is fast approaching, the way he or she reacts, how the process of dying progresses, and what the final moments are like. You may also recount the funeral or memorial service and describe the eulogy. Develop a story that—in following this person into the process of dying—emphasizes how the person's fears influence that process. Creating this story, in which the main character's fears of death are shaping the way he or she is to die, will provide you with a parable about the importance of coming to terms with such fears and perhaps some clues about how to come to terms with them yourself.

Peg's Fable

"The old hag cowers in the darkest corner of her hut, glaring with red-rimmed eyes at the creeping shadows. Within each pulsating, flickering shadow is the essence of some evil deed she herself has perpetrated. Prowling the wall, approaching her corner, is the ghost of her spite, lusting for blood. Groans of anguish fall from the ceiling—voices echoing her malicious gossip, her slandering of neighbors, her vilifying others' honest efforts. Greed sits in the hag's chair, lapping up a beggar's meager meal to feed its soft bulging belly.

"Her breath comes with the rasp of curses cast at thriving children, blighting them. The stench of pride, acrid as burning hair, fills the room. The hag feels bowel-emptying terror; the greasy skin of her back raises stiff quills of gray hair in dread. Death is at the door, and these memories are but Death's lackeys, come to torment the dying hag with the dregs of her life.

"The hag falls to her knees as Death enters the hut. Death comes as an open black mouth, filled with shark's teeth and a bitter purple tongue. Its pallid lips reach out for her as if she were a morsel on a fork. The hag screams and buries her head, too frightened to bargain or confess repentance. One flick of the fearfully livid tongue and she is devoured. The shadows of greed and slander and hate caper in her empty room, unexorcised."

Robert's Fable

Robert wrote his death fable the week after the terrible earthquake in Armenia. Survivors were still being rescued after being buried alive for ten days. One vivid news account told of a woman, trapped under the rubble with her young daughter for over a week, who made incisions in her skin with a piece of broken glass so her dehydrated daughter could suck her blood. Robert could not stop dwelling on such accounts, and they provided the setting for his death fable.

"Robchinko Ryzhkov was on the phone in his third-story office in Leninakan when the tremor began to build. Within two seconds he was under his desk. First a moment of respite—then the heavy desk was sliding across the room, rudely pushing him along with it. All at once he heard a deafening sound as the walls shook apart. Suddenly the floor was giving way. When he awoke, all was dark. He did not know where he was, only that his head hurt, he could not move his right leg, and he was pinned under something large, cold, and hard, perhaps four inches above him. Imprisoned on his back, he was unable to move.

"At first he thought he was in a dream. Then he caught an image of having dived under his desk, and in a moment of stark horror, he realized that this was very real. He screamed for help. All was silence. He screamed and screamed and screamed and screamed. He pushed with all his strength at the fallen beam that was pinning him. There was no give. He tried to wriggle out from under it. His right leg was hopelessly tangled in something he could neither see nor reach with his hands. Again he screamed and screamed and screamed until his screams had worn down to a soft moan.

"Then came the realization that he might slowly die in this terrible manner. More alone than he'd ever felt, his mind grew dark with terror. Hearing a shriek well up from deep inside, he could not think. Because he was unable to collect himself, he could not pay his last silent respects to the life he had lived or to those he had loved. And he could not attempt to come to peace with his fate. He was suspended in panic for endless hours. He began going in and out of nightmarish fits of sleep. Before passing out for the final time, he was still wearing an expression of horror and dread as he fought desperately to maintain consciousness and stay in his body."

With these three personal rituals, culminating in the morbid endings of their death fables, Peg and Robert have been rattling their systems of death denial. They have uncovered deep fears about death and looked at them directly. In the following stage of the program, they will be exploring ways they can more effectively deal with and begin to transcend such fears. You too will be guided to shift your focus toward a constructive response to the fears you have identified up to this point in the program.

THE SECOND STAGE:
Transcending the Fear of Death

"Man is poised midway between the gods and the beasts," observed the ancient Roman philosopher Plotinus. Ken Wilber explains that even if evolution is bringing us up from the beasts and toward the gods, being poised midway presents a terrible dilemma. The beasts are mortal, but they do not know it. The gods are immortal, and they know it. "But poor man, up from beasts and not yet a god, was that unhappy mixture: he was mortal, and he knew it."[1] With every evolutionary step toward greater intelligence, humanity became more aware of its "mortal and death-stained fate."

A question that divides people is whether we are more like the beasts or more like the gods in relation to our mortality. For some, it is intuitively obvious that we all perish as beasts, and that is the end of the story. For others, it is just as intuitively obvious that an aspect of who we are, an essence perhaps referred to as the soul, lives on after physical death. The evidence for each side of the argument is open to interpretation, and each of us is left, finally, to decide around which orientation we organize our understanding of life and death. But whether one takes great comfort in one's idea of heaven or other vision of an afterlife, is terrified by images of a demon-infested hell, or is quite certain that there is no afterlife, the quest for "symbolic immortality," in Robert Jay Lifton's terms,[2] seems to be a motivating force in most people's psyches.

Lifton describes five modes for attempting to transcend death by achieving symbolic immortality. The first is biological immortality, epitomized by family continuity and imagery of an endless biological chain linked to one's sons and daughters, their offspring, and on and on into eternity. A second mode for attaining symbolic immortality is through one's creative contributions, which may live on "through great works of art, literature, or science, or through more humble influences on people around us."[3] Here we take comfort in the knowledge that our best efforts may become part of human continuity. A third mode of symbolic immortality involves an identity with nature, a knowledge that the natural world will survive our physical demise, and that we, from dust to dust, will be returned to that natural world.

A fourth mode of transcending death involves a belief in "a specific concept of life after death, not only as a form of 'survival' but even as a release from the profane burdens of life into a higher plane of existence." Lifton believes that the "common thread in all great religions is the spiritual quest and realization of the hero-founder that enables him to confront and transcend death and to provide a model for generations of believers to do the same . . . . One is offered the opportunity to be reborn into a timeless realm of ultimate, death-transcending truths."[4]

Lifton's fifth mode, "experiential transcendence," is based on an inner experience that is "so intense and all-encompassing that time and space disappear [and there is] a sense of extraordinary psychic unity, and perceptual intensity, and of ineffable illumination and insight."[5] William James examined the impact of such experiences and reported that "mystical states of a well-pronounced and emphatic sort *are* usually authoritative over those who have them . . . . Mystical experiences are as direct perceptions of fact for those who have them as any sensations ever were for us."[6] We will focus on the concept of experiential transcendence, and its provocative implications for our understanding of death, in the third stage of this program.

Stop here and reflect in your journal on the concept of "symbolic immortality." How do you see the quest for symbolic immortality operating in people you know? How is it at play in your own life? Do you have sons or daughters who will carry your biological inheritance from your parents into the future? What will live on in the world in terms of your accomplishments or influence on others? In what ways are you able to take comfort in your connection with the natural world and your knowledge that the natural world will continue after your physical being has reunited with it? What beliefs or concepts, religious or otherwise, do you hold that give comfort or meaning regarding death and what follows it? Does it make intuitive sense to you that these means of attaining symbolic immortality can lead to greater peace and meaning during the limited time you do have here on Earth?

In this second stage of the program, you are presented with three more personal rituals. The first is designed to help you further analyze your fears regarding death for the purpose of taking steps to face them more effectively. In the second, you will be exploring "sacred time" and symbolic immortality. The third ritual involves the creation of another death fable, this one portraying your vision of a person who has come into peace with death.

PERSONAL RITUAL 7: LOOKING FEAR IN THE TEETH

Anxiety, Yalom notes, can be a "guide as well as enemy and can point the way to authentic existence."[7] He emphasizes that while anxiety can be used to increase awareness, it is critical to be able to reduce it to manageable levels when facing one of the mature adult's major tasks: coming to terms with "the reality of decline and diminishment."[8] A strategy Yalom advocates for reducing anxiety is to name it and explore it, as you have been doing in the previous rituals, and to break it down into component fears, as you will be doing in this one. He explains that a fear that "can neither be understood nor located cannot be confronted and becomes more terrible still: it begets a feeling of helplessness which invariably generates further anxiety."[9] But he offers the assurance that it

> is a matter of no small importance that one be able to explain and order the events in our lives into some coherent and predictable pattern. To name something, to locate its place in a causal sequence, is to begin to experience it as under our control. . . . The sense of potency that flows from understanding

occurs even in the matter of our basic existential situation: each of us feels less futile, less helpless, and less alone, even when, ironically, what we come to understand is the fact that each of us is basically helpless and alone.[10]

Thus Yalom encourages a "rational analysis" of death anxiety to sort out the various component fears, the major strategy being "to separate ancillary *feelings* of helplessness from the true helplessness that issues from facing one's unalterable existential situation."[11] Among the components of fear he enumerates are the pain of dying, the fear of an afterlife and the unknown, concern for one's family, fear for one's body, loneliness and regression, and the fact that "in achievement-oriented Western countries death is curiously equated with failure." He stresses that "each of these component fears, examined separately and rationally, is less frightening than the entire gestalt."[12] After discussing ways that people can exert tangible control over circumstances that affect their health and quality of life, such as when they involve themselves in social action or "discover with exhilaration that they can elect not to do the things they do not wish to do," he notes that "when all else seems beyond one's control, one, even then, has the power to control one's attitude toward one's fate."[13]

In this ritual, you will be selecting one, two, or three of the most troubling fears or areas of anxiety you identified in the earlier rituals. Recognizing them as components of your fear of death, you will discuss, in your journal, the steps you can take to approach them with understanding and a sense of mastery. Review your experiences to this point in the program and identify your most significant fears. Use each of them as a heading in your journal, and under each heading, explore the following three questions about each fear:

To what assumptions is it linked?

What are the probabilities that the fearful circumstances will occur?

What can I do to decrease their likelihood or intensity?

Complete the ritual by discussing what you have written in your journal with at least one person who cares about you.

Peg's Analysis

Reflecting on the assumptions she linked to her fears of aging and illness, Peg wrote, "Sickness and old age are times of diminished power. Without power, there is no dignity. Thus dignity can be eroded by physical circumstances." As to the probabilities of the fearful circumstances occurring: "They are pretty high, judging by the general population, and if I want to put my faith in statisticians. Mitigation would be to stay in good health, die sooner, or somehow find internal resources greater than the provocations of my worst-case scenario. Maybe the dementia of old age is merciful. When Hilda broke her hip in the nursing home, she believed she'd stumbled over a bale of hay in her goat barn. In a real way *she* wasn't in the nursing home at all."

Reflecting on what she could do to decrease the likelihood or intensity of her fears coming to fruition, Peg offered herself the following advice: "Live well. Stay active. Be attentive to my body's needs. Take care of my spirit. Let my friends and family know what I want. Trust. Plan a decent way out if I don't like the hand I'm dealt. Practice visualizations so that I have somewhere to go if I'm ever trapped in that hospital bed. Be cunning. Be wise. Be trusting of the ultimate good that comes from all adversity. Breathe."

Robert's Analysis

Robert reflected on how the fear of being maimed was such a strong element in his death anxiety. "That sure breaks down one important component of my fear of death. Giving more attention to the fear of being maimed separates it out, gives me a chance to see where I can exert some control over that potential fate. First, it is helpful to know that it is a potential fate, not a certain fate. And it is also important to know that it is a fate that does happen to people—and to 'look it in the teeth' by accepting that it could happen to me. 'There but for fortune.'

"I'm starting to see how, when others are struck by tragedy, my response gets all entangled in my fears. I try to shield myself from what happened, to emotionally distance myself from people who have been badly injured. I'm embarrassed that I haven't 'found the time' to pay a call on Neil Johnson since his accident. Part of it is I was just afraid of the awkwardness—I didn't know what to say. Maybe I'd better figure out what to say. Maybe I'd better deal a little more realistically with my own terror of losing an arm or the ability to walk.

"I'm reminded of that meditation retreat at which the Vietnamese holy man [Thich Nhat Hanh] talked about how the suffering we see around us provides an opportunity to develop the compassion that the Buddhists think of as the noblest emotion. Instead of responding to others' misfortune with fear or pity or guilt—all of which create distance—he teaches that we can turn such events into opportunities to practice opening our hearts, to know our oneness with all other beings. It seemed kind of abstract at the retreat, but it is making more sense to me now. I liked the blessing he did before meals: after appreciating the aesthetic beauty of the food, you take a moment to feel compassion—*not* guilt—toward all those who could not enjoy such a meal this day. Maybe to recognize the 'there but for fortune' aspect of my compassion for others who are struck by tragedy would make me a bigger person regarding such matters and better prepare me for whatever is to be. Perhaps it would be very good for me—not just an obligation or a courtesy—to hear through my own ears what the struggle has been like for Neil. It might even be a good 'emotional inoculation' to hear the gory details of his accident, of what it was like for him to learn of his losses, and to hear with an open heart his struggle to come to terms with them.

"I can do other things about my fear of mutilation as well. I can't prevent an airplane crash or act of senseless violence, but I can take appropriate precautions and operate with greater awareness that much of what I value and take such pleasure in is fragile. If I can raise this to the level of acting with appreciation for the blessings I have,

I think it will make for a much better attitude. Also, by maintaining an awareness of the fragility of what I value, I will live so that if I am seriously injured, I at least don't have to blame it on my own stupidity. I guess there are some situations in which I would take major risks, but even there, a tragedy would be different if I were making a free and conscious choice.

"And, of course, there's the 'count your blessings' part of the issue. The awareness that a sudden and terrible downward shift in the quality of my life could be around any corner reminds me, again, of the preciousness of the moment. It particularly makes me want to spend more quality time with Dawn, more time in nature, and more time with good music and good books. I don't know why I don't sink into those cherished spaces more often. 'Too busy' seems lame in the face of Neil's plight."

You can see Robert struggling with his recognition that he would be well served to "sink into those cherished spaces more often" and his awareness that he doesn't. Later he will be challenged to take effective steps to change this pattern.

PERSONAL RITUAL 8: A VIEW OF "SYMBOLIC IMMORTALITY" THROUGH SACRED TIME

Many spiritual traditions make a distinction between *ordinary time* and *sacred time*. Sacred time is not of the clock but of the heart. To be lost in wonderment watching a sunrise is to enter sacred time. Sometimes we will awake from an inspiring dream and sense we have been in sacred time. One of the most enchanting qualities of love is its ability to transport us from our workaday world into sacred time. Inward-focused practices, such as prayer and meditation, can also be routes into sacred time. An observation, made by the great historian of religion Mircea Eliade, worth remembering for its hopefulness, is that the sacred often bursts forth at the darkest hour, purifying and reordering the individual and the world.[14] We encourage you here to use the following guided imagery instructions as a gateway to sacred time.

Prepare by creating an atmosphere that brings you comfort and inspiration. Use candles, soft lighting, inspiring art, and any other objects that might enhance the experience for you. Shield the space from interruptions such as phone calls. Consider having spiritually uplifting music playing in the background as the instructions are read into your tape or as you create an experience that accomplishes the intent of the ritual. Have your journal, death shield, and colored markers nearby. Arrange to perform this ritual in a mood receptive to entering sacred time. Deep relaxation, meditation, or aerobic exercise such as running, swimming, or free-form dancing can help open such a space. When you are ready to begin, find a comfortable position, take a deep breath, and close your eyes.

The path you will be following into sacred time is marked by physical relaxation and uplifting memories. Settle in comfortably—finding an inner quiet, peace, and warmth. [Pause.] Thank your body for its hard work and good service. [Pause.] Find the parts of your body that need special attention, healing, or rest. Picture a warm, wise hand filled with fragrant ointment gently touching and appreciating those parts. [Pause.] Focus your attention and sense the melting, calming relaxation that comes into those sore and tired places. [30-second pause.] As you focus on my voice, other sounds fade away. All is well with you for this journey into sacred time. You are always free to return to ordinary consciousness by simply opening your eyes and exhaling fully, and you are just as free to explore the riches of your inner world. You will recall all you need of this experience, and you will emerge from it with insight and power. You can move and adjust yourself at any time, yawning and stretching, rearranging until your body is peaceful and satisfied.

Begin to reflect on the holiest, most sacred times of your past. [Pause.] Remember a moment of shared love. [Pause.] Recall seeing a newborn child. [Pause.] You have felt yourself awed by a sunset, a waterfall, or the seashore. [Pause.] You have heard inspiring music [pause]; seen great art [pause]; savored a creative breakthrough [pause]; sat in an awe-inspiring cathedral or other place of reverence. [Pause.] Focus on a time that was particularly inspiring. [Pause.] Recall it vividly. [Pause.] Relive it in each of your senses. Breathe into the vision [pause], the sounds [pause], the feelings [pause]. Let go into the memory. [20-second pause.] Soon you will hear counting, from one to seven. When you hear the number seven, you will be fully relaxed and deep in sacred time.

One. As you bask in the inspiring feelings of the scene you have remembered, the healing hand sensitively massages your back, shoulders, and neck. You sigh, content.

Two. The healing hand moves to your face, massaging your forehead, eyes, cheeks, scalp, mouth, and jaw. Each breath fills your awareness. Unhurried, your sense of sacred time deepens.

Three. The muscles and joints of your arms and legs are rejuvenated by the healing hand. You exhale fully, feeling vitally alive and relaxed.

Four. The healing hand finds wounded or weary parts in the trunk of your body—pelvis, hips, buttocks, genitals, stomach, spine, ribs, heart—nourishing them with tender touch.

Five. The healing hand continues to touch away your pains as you exhale your tiredness, hurt, and disillusion. Your breathing is deep and pleasurable.

Six. Fully relaxed, you notice a pleasant tingling on your skin. As you smile, you feel a deep sense of peacefulness.

Seven. Your heart is open. You are absorbed in the comfortable, warm sensations. Your breathing fills the moment. You have entered sacred time. [20-second pause.]

Continuing to breathe deeply, watch your breath rising and falling. [Pause.] Your mind is clear as you savor the heightened awareness of this open moment. [60-second pause.]

From this heightened awareness, you find a sense of peace about life and about death. It is possible to find much to appreciate about your life and to take pleasure in who you are. [Pause.] Recall your earlier reflections on your relationship with "symbolic immortality." What attitudes *or activities give your life the greatest meaning? [30-second pause.]*

You are also, from this space, able to glimpse other attitudes or activities that would offer greater fulfillment and a more viable sense of "symbolic immortality." Let yourself become aware of attitudes and actions that could make your life richer. [20-second pause.] Now imagine yourself living from these attitudes or carrying out these activities. [Pause.] See, feel, and sense yourself living in a way that will give you greater peace about your existence and greater meaning to your mortality. [Pause]. Breathe fully into this experience. Enjoy it. [60-second pause.]

Focus on a sensation in your body that relates to living a life that is satisfying and fulfilling. Identify the part of your body where this sensation is most intense. Find the shape of the sensation—notice its borders. [Pause.] See its color. [Pause.] Explore its texture. [Pause.] In a moment, you will recognize a symbol emerging out of these shapes and colors that represents living with a profound sense of peace.

Watch as the symbol appears. [Pause.] You may actually see the symbol take form, or you may simply sense what it is. It will further evolve over the next few moments. Relax as it becomes increasingly clear. [20-second pause.]

As a fitting symbol of this richer way of living emerges, prepare to draw it on your shield. [Pause.] Take several deep breaths and begin to stretch your body. [20-second pause.] Open your eyes and draw the symbol on the portion of your shield that is labeled "Transcending Death Anxiety." As you draw this symbol, you may find that it is changing even as you are creating it or that you have more than one image to draw. Draw whatever comes. When you have completed your drawing, you will find that you have returned to full waking consciousness, feeling refreshed, confident, and able to effectively and creatively meet the requirements of your day.

In your journal, under a heading called "My View Through Sacred Time," describe your experience. Reflect particularly on the means of symbolic immortality you reviewed and the new attitudes and actions you explored. How did these look from sacred time?

How do they seem to you now? Reflect on the meaning of the new symbol or symbols you drew on your death shield. Consider using the creative projection technique for further examining their personal significance. "Become" the symbol, as you did earlier, and, in first-person present tense, describe yourself as that symbol.

Peg's View Through Sacred Time

In thinking about ways she could embrace a sense of death transcendence, Peg wrote, "My life is filled with meaning. It matters that I work as I do with people. My writing has meaning. My family relationships are meaningful. I have precious friends. My connection to The Land [a large forest tract in the Coast Range of Oregon, with the Yaquina River running through it, for which she and her husband are steward-owners] is sacred. I use my mind and experience well. I have not lost my sense of wonder and surprise. I find it easy to appreciate. I love to learn and to craft beautiful objects and artful phrases.

"I have adult offspring. They are neither 'mine' nor 'children.' They survive well and show promise of continuing growth. I was a factor in their being. I have been a good teacher, often by my blunders, impetuousness, and intransigence but sometimes by intent as well. Ah, the natural world—that is my home, my sanctuary—it is where I belong. I know that. I'll be planted there, dissolved, reabsorbed, reborn. Or at least my chemicals will. I believe this is not a wasteful or a random universe. I believe in meaning and intent. I do not know the pattern of which my life is a part, but I believe that the synchronicities of being are too frequent to be chance. Something is in charge. Something knows. I've had numinous moments and dreams; there *is* sacred time and sacred space. The only difficulty is slowing down enough to enter them."

Peg's symbol for "transcending death anxiety" was a fallen fir giant in the forest. She reflected, "It is a 'nurse log.' In its death it becomes shelter and food for other life forms. Fungi grow on it, reducing its coarse cellulose to a finer form, the better to rot back into the earth.

The creek it partially dams flows over it, aerating the water for the fish and crawdads. Baby cedars take root in the moss of its bark, sinking their root tendrils deep into its body. The hollow core that caused it to fall becomes the home for a raccoon family. Beetles thrive under its bark. Wind-blown soil collects in the crevices, and bird-sown seed sprouts huckleberry bushes. Slugs and ferns find habitat. A heron perches on its submerged branches, alert for scuttling crawdads lurking in the shallows. Bacteria, beetles, mushrooms, and fungi digest it and live their lives in vital harmony with death. In the great pan of its upturned rootball, stones caged in roots see the light of day, and the soil erodes, enriching the river. There is no waste here."

Robert's View Through Sacred Time

"The memory I went to when I scanned my experiences with sacred time was powerful. It was Dawn's twenty-fifth birthday. We weren't certain yet that we would be life partners—there were so many other things we each needed to work out before we could make that commitment. I had invited her to my home for dinner. She arrived to candlelight and twenty-five presents—from trinkets to treasures—hidden Easter-egg style throughout the apartment. After a very special dinner, we spent the evening with her searching for a gift, opening it, and then being told there was still one more. After the fourth or fifth gift, and all the way up to her birthday number, she would look at me incredulously each time or squeal with childlike delight as she eagerly set out to find the next surprise. The whole evening was a prolonged high. I savored her enthusiasm as she opened each gift. Her expressions of pleasure and appreciation seemed so real and heartfelt that every gift deepened our bond. I took pleasure in having found gifts that really pleased her, and I could tell that she felt appreciated and deeply recognized in the selections I had made.

"In the exercise, I realized that although I've never looked at that birthday, memorable though it was, as a milestone, it really was. I think we made a commitment to each other in the ethers that night. Although it was only after separations and years that we came to merge our lives together, I had the sense that something very spiritual had occurred between us that evening. In the midst of this thought, I felt suddenly uplifted into what I think of as a spiritual feeling. It's hard to describe, but it gives me a glimpse of what words like *awe* and *rapture* can mean.

"Answering the question about what I do that best prepares me to come to terms with my mortality was simple. I was doing it right at that moment. By bringing back memories of the intensely loving moments Dawn and I shared on her twenty-fifth birthday, I was transported into a wonderful sense of joy and peace. In response to the question of what I could do more of, nothing made greater sense than to protect the time and create the atmosphere so I could go into this sacred space more frequently. It's clear to me from my memory of Dawn's birthday that love is a major point of entry into that spirit world."

From this account, we get an intimate view of Robert gaining greater sensitivity to deep but subtle longings as he reawakens to realms of his being that he considers "spiritual." On his death shield he drew a picture of the candlelit room. He found that by meditating on it, he could recapture the ethereal feelings to which his memory of the experience had brought him in the exercise.

PERSONAL RITUAL 9: A SECOND DEATH FABLE,
"DEATH IN THE LIGHT OF TRANSCENDENCE"

You are about to write a second death fable. It will begin in the same setting and will portray the same main character and the same impending death as your first death fable, but in this story, the person has found some effective ways of transcending the fear of death. These happen, in fact, to be the same ways of living that you imagined in the previous personal ritual, when you viewed life and death through sacred time. In this story you will be exploring the difference in the dying process between one who is leading with the fear of death and one who is leading with peace and acceptance. A pioneer of family therapy, Virginia Satir, in her parting message to friends, colleagues, and family, said, "I send my love. Please support me in my passage to a new life." She thanked them for playing a significant part in the development of her ability to love: "As a result, my life has been rich and full, so I leave feeling very grateful." The main character of your death fable is to have found as much peace about dying as is reflected in Virginia Satir's statement.

Like the first death fable, this story will describe the way the main character first learns that death is fast approaching, his or her reactions, how the process of dying progresses, and what the final moments are like. You may also include a funeral or a eulogy. The two stories will be a study in contrasts regarding the dying process, dramatizing the effects of changing a single variable. In the second story, the central character has come into a peace that transcends death, as contrasted with the immobilizing fear portrayed in the first death fable. After reading Peg's and Robert's stories, again begin by relaxing in a comfortable spot and contemplating the death fable you are about to create. Allow your story to emerge from deep within you.

Peg's Second Death Fable

"The old midwife-herbalist sits by the fire, her weary body leaning doggedly to her task. Before her is a vellum book, thick and substantial. Holding her goose quill pen, she copies down the years of her learnings. She writes of healings and losses, of children born and mothers dead. She draws pictures of herbs in bloom and signs to watch for in harvesting them. In the margin of her book she writes a jest at herself, to bring a smile to the reader who will inherit her wisdom.

"The room darkens. The candle flickers, and the air cools. The midwife looks up. Death, a long-familiar ally, is coming through the door carrying a lamb's wool blanket to warm and cradle her. She smiles in recognition and draws a last flourish under the final entry in her Life Book. In the shadows, mercy and curiosity and service circle close to calm her heart and quiet her breath. A smile comes as she folds inward, her work complete.

"The funeral is attended by those she's healed and taught, all telling stories of her goodness and humor and telling how they themselves are the better for her having lived. They mark her grave with four redwood trees at the cardinal points and a thousand daffodil bulbs; then they set in place a forest of wind chimes and prisms that sing in the night and flash rainbow light in the daytime."

Robert's Second Death Fable

"Once Robchinko Ryzhkov realized that his fate was sealed, he ceased his frantic digging, and a sense of peace fell over him. He knew he had done all he could to free himself from the rubble. He knew he could not. And he knew his time was very limited. 'This is when a review of my life is supposed to flash in front of me,' he thought, but it did not, so he began the review in his mind. He saw how his life had directed him toward certain lessons. He took satisfaction in how much he had learned, and he noted his failures, accepting that the time to right them had passed. He remembered particularly the most loving moments along the way. Those seemed to be the important landmarks from this vantage point. As he began to say good-bye to those whom he had loved the most, the tears seemed to pour out endlessly from deep in his being. Finally, he directed his attention toward his faith that his life and death were part of a larger plan. He realized that this was perhaps his hardest moment ever for maintaining faith in a good and greater Power. He willed himself to imagine a light beyond, like he'd read about, and he fell asleep with that image in his mind. In his dream, a beautiful, ornate, horse-driven carriage was taking him above the clouds and toward that light. He never returned."

In the first stage of the program, Peg and Robert uncovered and examined their fears concerning death. In this stage, they each explored ways of contending with those fears, and they formulated ideas and images that might help them transcend them. Their second death fables each ended on a note opposite to that in their fables about "death in the shadow of fear." In the following stage of the program, you will watch as they strive for a reconciliation between the fear of death and the possibilities of transcending that fear, and you will be invited to also find a path toward such reconciliation.

THE THIRD STAGE:
A Confrontation Between the Fear of Death and Images of Transcending Death

We are physical beings, and we know without question that the body through which we experience life will one day die. We are also conscious beings, but we are not so certain about the fate of our awareness after the death of our body. Does all consciousness cease with physical death, or does some aspect of who we are live on, independent of the body?

You can probably find in yourself some support for each possibility. It may seem gut-wrenchingly obvious that the consciousness rooted in the body will cease to be when the body is no more. At the same time, the part of you that dreams and imagines and is capable of love and reverie may intuit that it has a life of its own beyond the body. This seeming contradiction about what happens after a person dies is not only a core religious question but also a central dilemma for the psyche. Freud argued that the conscious ego cannot conceive of *not* existing.

The answers we come to about what happens after death are a subtle yet emphatic force in shaping our values and the direction our lives will take. Ernest Becker identified, for instance, an integral relationship between the hoarding of wealth and power that blights much of civilization and the attempt to psychologically deny the reality of death: "All this seemingly useless surplus, dangerously and painstakingly wrought . . . goes to the very heart of human motivation, the urge to . . . transcend the limitations of the human condition and achieve victory over impotence and finitude."[1]

Such "symbolic immortality projects," tragic in their consequences, ultimately fail to offer peace in the face of our deepest questions and fears. Working out the issues internally and consciously, rather than projecting them onto one's world and unconsciously acting them out, demands greater skill and inner strength but also promises a more life-affirming resolution. The rituals in this part of the program highlight core issues in approaching our deepest conflicts about what ensues after physical death, and they provide guidance for addressing those issues.

Perhaps the most enigmatic question about death is what happens after we die. "Perchance to dream"—perhaps awareness survives the body—is the "rub" that prevents Hamlet from taking his own life, though "in my soul, 'tis bitter cold and I am sick at heart":

> But that the dread of something after death,
> The undiscovered country from whose bourn
> No traveler returns, puzzles the will,
> And makes us rather bear those ills we have,
> Than fly to others that we know not of.

The nature of that "undiscovered country" from which "no traveler returns" is an ultimate concern of most spiritual and religious systems, but until recently, with the documentation of various puzzling "near-death" phenomena—where the traveler actually does seem to return[2]—science has not attempted to address it. Stanislav and Christina Grof summarize the range of accounts of the world's religious, philosophical, and spiritual systems, ancient and modern, on the question:

> Dying is sometimes seen as a step up in the spiritual or cosmological hierarchy, a promotion into the world of revered ancestors, powerful spirits or demigods, or as a transition from the complicated earthly life fraught with suffering and problems to a blissful existence in the solar region or the realms of gods. More frequently the concept of afterlife involves dichotomies and polarities; there are hells and purgatories as well

as celestial realms and paradisiacal states. The posthumous journey of the soul is understood as a complex and difficult one. It is therefore essential to be well prepared when death comes. At the very least, it is necessary to acquire a knowledge of the cartography and laws of the afterlife existence.[3]

Many of humanity's most luminous moral and spiritual leaders throughout history taught about a dimension of consciousness that is eternal.[4] A glimpse from a different angle comes from the "life-after-life" reports of people who return from a close brush with death. Following such dramatic experiences, people often recall having had so unmistakable an encounter with a "Being of Light" and with an afterlife that the existence of each is beyond question for them. These conclusions appear to emerge independent of any prior religious or spiritual beliefs.[5] While increasingly well-documented reports about the "brilliant light that doesn't hurt the eyes [and] that surrounds one with a sense of profound love and wisdom," have become a staple of "New Age" thought, it is interesting to note the instruction that has been offered since the eighth century B.C. by the Buddhist *Bardo Thödal* (the *Tibetan Book of the Dead*): "Do not be frightened or bewildered by the luminous, brilliant, very sharp and clear light of supreme wisdom . . . be drawn to it . . . take refuge in it."

Research on people who have had a life-after-life encounter reveals that after the experience, they frequently enjoy a greater appreciation of other people and of their own lives and become less materialistic, less concerned with pleasing others, and more concerned with ultimate questions such as the meaning of life. These changes are often lasting. Perhaps most remarkably, they "enjoy an overwhelming increase in self-confidence, security, and self-esteem."[6] Other documentation lending support to the belief that consciousness survives after death includes the accumulation of increasingly authenticated reports of "past-life memories" and of clinical breakthroughs after such "memories" emerge.[7] Particularly impressive are the "memories" of children, as young as two or three, who in describing a past life are able to speak a language that is unknown in their locality or provide verifiable details about people and places to whom they could have had no exposure.[8]

These reports do not, however, in any scientifically acceptable manner, "prove" the existence of life after death.[9] The implications of near-death phenomena are still being fervently debated. The above discussion is presented not to persuade you that the case for an afterlife has been established but to offer some current views in humanity's enduring attempts to overcome the instinctual terror of death and to fulfill its yearning for an everlasting identity with the cosmos. We are suggesting, in fact, that on whichever side of the mortality-immortality debate you may align yourself, the debate continues to be waged at some level of your psyche. As long as humans are "poised midway between the gods and the beasts," deep conflict about the question will persist. The issues involved are central to your understanding of life as well as death. You are, in some part of your being, continually dealing with them, and we believe the act of bringing this inner dialogue into awareness and mindfully participating in it can yield substantial psychological benefits. That is the purpose of the following personal rituals. By focusing your awareness on this underlying psychic conflict, you will be cultivating a more viable and empowering mythology regarding death and life.

PERSONAL RITUAL 10: A DIALOGUE BETWEEN YOUR FEAR OF DEATH AND THE PROSPECT OF TRANSCENDING DEATH

In this ritual, you will personify, in a role-play, both your fear of death and the greatest peace about death that you can imagine. The character portraying your fear of death is in vivid contact with the biological terror of annihilation. The character personifying an acceptance of death is aware that some of the wisest and most illuminated individuals in humanity's history have found emotionally and intellectually viable ways of transcending that terror and takes heart in their example. The two characters will engage in debate and dialogue about their differences. You will, for this dramatization, physically enact each character. You will, in sequence, speak for one of them and then the other.

Prime yourself for representing the first character by reviewing your exploration of "the fear of death at its foundation," the "death fear" symbol on your shield, and your fable about "death in the shadow of fear." Contemplate the fears that are the most troubling to you. Prepare yourself to represent the other character by reviewing the perspective you gained as you viewed mortality through "sacred time," the symbolism on the portion of your shield called "Transcending Death Anxiety," and your fable about "death in the light of transcendence." Recall the modes for death transcendence or symbolic immortality that seemed the most gratifying or plausible for you. The two sides will be taking part in a debate. On one side will be the primal, animalistic part of you that is terrified of death and annihilation. Facing it will be the voice of intuitions and beliefs you hold or find most palatable regarding peace about death and the prospects for transcendence of death.

Allow yourself to explore the two sides of the issue by alternately identifying fully with each position. For each side, invent a character or use the character from one of your death fables, and create a role-play. Find physical postures that depict the life stance represented by each side. Wholeheartedly dramatize the dialogue. The impact of this exercise may be increased if someone whom you trust and who cares about your personal development serves as a witness. The presence of another can both affirm and ritualize your experience. The person can later share observations and impressions. New insights about the relationship between your fears of death and your hopes of transcending them may emerge from reviewing the exchange. If you do not arrange to have a partner, you can use a tape recorder to serve as witness. Familiarize yourself with the following instructions. They end with a summary that can guide you as you proceed.

The first step is to find a physical posture that expresses your fear of death. Move into the posture and experiment with it. Find a fitting facial expression. Should you grimace, scowl, frown, stare, twitch? What kind of gestures would be most appropriate for this character? Will you point? Put your hands in your pocket? Hug yourself? Shake nervously? Dance? Jump? Pray? Crawl?

Once you have found a posture for the first character, become acquainted with the other character in a similar manner. Take two steps forward, turn around, and "face" your first character. Move into a posture that portrays peace about death. Experiment until you find the most fitting gestures and facial expression. Establishing this character is a drill in sensing your way beyond primal, fearful images about death. Give yourself all the time you need.

After establishing the postures and facial expressions that best represent each character, move back and forth a few times, becoming familiar with the roles. Require each character to observe and size up the other. Finally, allow a dialogue to begin.

In the initial interchanges, highlight the differences between the two characters. You can begin the dialogue by stepping into the position of one of the characters, finding its posture, and making a statement that reflects this character's basic stance regarding life and death. Speak while looking at and reacting to the other character. Be conscious of using an apt tone of voice. Find the words that express your feelings and thoughts as this character. Then step into the other position and respond. Keep your facial expressions, posture, gestures, and tones appropriate to the character you are portraying. As the two characters encounter each other, allow the words to flow unrehearsed. Keep the dialogue going without long pauses or planning. Trust your spontaneous comments. Continue to move physically between the two characters as you let the dialogue develop.

In the early part of the dialogue, you will be exploring where the two sides hold incompatible beliefs, values, or feelings. Eventually, you will be attempting to establish improved communication between the characters. If the dialogue gets bogged down, have one side ask the other, "What do you want of me?" Provide a thoughtful response. Have each character listen with increasing care and compassion to the other's position.

In summary, (1) find the posture and gestures of each side and experiment in moving from one to the other; (2) give words to one side so the character can make a clear opening statement, then move to the position of the other side and begin with a clear opening statement; and (3) let the dialogue develop. Read the following accounts of Peg's and Robert's dialogues and then begin your own.

Excerpts from Peg's Dialogue

Peg's dialogue was between the Hag and the Healer from her death fables.

HAG: Goody-goody!

HEALER: Goody-goody! Me?

HAG: You! Thinking that if you're just good enough, then dying will be okay. Fool! You need to gather more things and make yourself plump, the better to withstand the lean times.

HEALER: You really think that'll make you safe? I don't! I believe that being helpful is the answer, not riches, when Death comes.

HAG: Don't talk to me of Death! Death can't get me if I'm clever enough—I can hold him off indefinitely.

HEALER: Foolish old woman! Death is a soothing ointment on the scalded flesh; it is rest at the end of toil; it is a friend leading us into a bright place. And Death comes when it will, not at our bidding.

HAG: You'll sing a different tune when pain tears your guts and ideas elude your grasp. Better to wrap yourself in silk clothes, eat rich food, and drink wine before your throat closes forever.

HEALER: What of love?

HAG: Fairy tales! Fantasy!

HEALER: What if I rub your poor tired back and bring you a bowl of fresh vegetable soup? Let us tell stories of being young and juicy—will you laugh with me?

HAG: Rub my back? Where it aches? What will you charge?

HEALER: How about a smile and one sentence about the goodness of life?

HAG: A hard bargain.

HEALER: Oh, I'll rub you without it, but it's what I'd like most in barter. After all, fair's fair.

HAG: For a goody-goody, you're a tough cookie. All right. How's this for a smile?

HEALER: Not bad, but you could use some practice—happy eyes are part of a smile, you know, not just baring your teeth. Try again; it'll feel good. And don't forget the sentence . . .

HAG: You're right, it does feel good—how curious! Here's my sentence: Life is good when you're in touch—like now, with my back being rubbed.

HEALER: Wait until you rub mine! The big secret is that it feels better to give than receive, odd as that may seem to you right now. You'll get your chance.

Excerpts from Robert's Dialogue

"The fear side was huddled up in a fetal position, trembling, screaming, 'I don't want to die; I'm not ready to die.' On the other side was a big man—standing tall, breathing fully, and expanding into this space. He was very serene about the whole thing. He even exuded a strange kind of peace as he cryptically said to the trembling character, 'It is not death that you should fear.' The two began to speak with each other.

FEAR: What do you mean, implying that there are worse things to fear! I'm so fully consumed by my fear of death that I can't even get a handle on how to begin to contain it. And you want me to find something else to be afraid of!

PEACE: I'm not meaning to make light of your terror. I just want you to know that you would find comfort if you could grasp the full picture. You are part of a bigger plan. Death is but a doorway to the next stage. A glorious realm awaits you on the other side. Take peace in this knowledge.

FEAR: I don't experience death as anything but terrifying! I have no reason to believe in fantasies of another world, much less a "glorious" one. You're not going to create false hopes in me! I think the foundation of all your supposed inner peace is built on wishful thinking.

PEACE: You know, that's the basis of the whole debate. Someone full of fear, like you, sees everything teeming with danger and decline. Those who have been touched by the world of spirit have a different take. They still see the suffering, but they also see the opportunity to quell that suffering with a sense of deep connection to a larger plan. The question comes down to deciding which position to believe.

FEAR: That's no problem for me. I don't trust the wishful fantasies of the self-proclaimed spiritually evolved.

PEACE: Of course not. If you've not been touched by that realm, it's not very convincing. But you see, there is more than what you experience. I've had moments when I have been touched by a sense of spirit that is infinitely greater than what is encased in my body. It's not wishful thinking—it's direct experience. But when you hear such reports, however vivid and sincere, they are quickly discounted and forgotten.

FEAR: Why should I believe you?

PEACE: Which one of us is happier? You have to admit that between the two of us, I'm the one who's found serenity and joy. By my criteria, that merits a certain amount of authority. The kind of happiness that grows out of deep peace even in the midst of great distress is found in the saints, like Gandhi and Schweitzer. They all believed in, had direct knowledge of, the spiritual, death-transcending foundations of their lives.

FEAR: Hey, hearsay doesn't convince me. I'd like to be able to believe what you believe, but I can't find a shred of convincing evidence.

PEACE: Come here, Fear. Let me just hold you for a minute. Let my energy calm you. I'll hang out with you in your world until enough of me has rubbed off on you that you feel secure enough to venture into mine.

FEAR: What makes you think it is not I who will rub off on you? Just watch as your rose-colored glasses darken in my presence until you finally have to whip them off and gaze directly at the stark, terrifying truths of existence.

PEACE: There is no question for me that I am the one who is tuned into the eternal truths of existence. They are beyond your wavelength. But with those truths backing me, it is I who will rub off on you. You will be pleased.

FEAR (feeling mocked and mobilized for a fight): We'll just see who's going to rub off on whom . . ."

After completing your own dialogue, summarize it in your journal and reflect on the way these characters representing your relationship to death were able to communicate with each other. Were they able to inform each other or come to any resolution of their differences? We suggest that over the next several days you extend the dialogue with two or three more rounds of at least ten minutes each. Commit yourself to attaining greater integration between these two sides of your primal response to the fact of being mortal.

PERSONAL RITUAL 11: OPENING THE SPACE FOR A NEW INTEGRATION

In the previous ritual you consciously engaged in a dramatization of your conflict. In this one you will invite your unconscious mind to open itself to the conflict and help facilitate a resolution. You will be performing a ritual dance to open within yourself the space for a new and deeper integration between your primal fear of death and your intuited or acquired ways of transcending it. One way to open a space for new and creative insight is to temporarily put aside the concepts you currently hold, to more or less peek beneath them so you can freshly perceive the issue. In this ritual you will invite yourself to go deeper than the ideas about death you have been examining, to travel below your conscious mind and into the realm of your intuition and creative imagination.

You may have heard of the trance dance used in many tribal cultures to attain altered states of consciousness. In this ritual, you will also be using patterned movement to bring yourself into a preverbal state of openness and receptivity. Begin by selecting a piece of music with a fast beat and no lyrics. Rock music or percussion music with a tribal beat, such as "Totem" by Gabrielle Roth, "Drums of Passion" by Olatunji, or "At the Edge" by Mickey Hart, can serve the purpose.

With the music playing, stand in the position and posture of the character who symbolizes your fear of death. Explore the way this character dances to this music. Then move about ten feet across the room and into the posture of the other character. Explore this individual's dance. Once you have established the two separate dances, begin to move in a circle with the positions of the two characters being points on opposite sides of the circle. As you approach the position of one of the characters, allow your movements to become that character's movements. As you leave that position, release those movements and then find the movement patterns representing the other character. Go around the circle at least three times, alternating your movements as you reach each character. Finally, continuing to go around the circle, pick up speed and allow the movements to blend into a new movement belonging to neither the first character nor the second. As this occurs, begin to chant, out loud, "Let the change begin!" Allow the circle to become smaller until you have spiraled into its center. No longer spinning around, allow your movements to be free in their form.

For several more minutes, continue your movements while chanting, "Let the change begin!" Know that you are opening a space for new insight and a new relationship with the basic questions regarding your mortality. If different words want to come, allow them. Move to embody the words you are chanting. Feel them deeply. Move rapidly and emphatically to the beat. Continue until your body is tired and your mind is clear (if you have any physical limitations, pace yourself accordingly). Finally, lie down and immediately embark on Personal Ritual 12, following.

Here is a summary of the steps for initiating your trance dance: (1) establish the dance of each of your characters, placing them about ten feet apart; (2) move at least three times around a ten-foot circle, taking on the movement of each character as you approach its position; (3) picking up speed, allow the movements to blend into a new, unrehearsed pattern; (4) begin to chant, "Let the change begin!" as you begin to spiral in toward the center of the circle; (5) from the center, continue dancing freely, allowing your chant to evolve as it will; and (6) lie down, relax, and begin listening to the guided imagery instructions of the following personal ritual.

PERSONAL RITUAL 12: A BODY METAPHOR OF RESOLUTION

You will need to have familiarized yourself with this ritual or prepared a tape or made arrangements so someone can read it to you immediately after finishing your trance dance. With your journal, death shield, and markers nearby, feel your body calming as you focus your mind on these instructions.

Bring your attention to your breathing. [Pause.] Listen for and feel each in breath and each out breath. [Pause.] Notice how your stomach and chest fill . . . and empty. [Pause.] As you continue to breathe and relax, you are better able to concentrate on my voice and on the suggestions I will offer. If outside sounds or passing thoughts cross your mind, they fade quietly into the background just as they occur. Your breathing is slow and deep as you relax more completely with each of your next five breaths. One [pause]; two [pause]; three [pause]; four [pause]; five [pause].

Let one side of your body represent your primal fear of death. Sense if it is your left side or your right side. Do not pull back; there is vital information here for you to have. [Pause.] This side of your body is immersed in the energy of fear. It is reacting to your primal fear of death. As you tune into this frightened side of your body, an image that represents your fear of death may emerge. Give it some time, and if an image does appear, examine it. [20-second pause.] Focus again now on the feelings in this side of your body and explore your body's response to the energies and images of fear. [30-second pause.]

Imagine now that the other side of your body represents confidence, hope, and harmony about death. [Pause.] Focus on this side of your body. You may experience feelings of acceptance or tranquility. As you tune into this more peaceful side of your body, an image that represents serenity about dying may emerge. Give it some time, and if an image does appear, examine it. [20-second pause.] Focus again now on the feelings in this side of your body and explore your body's response to the energies and images of peace and serenity. [30-second pause.]

Compare the sensations between these two sides of your body. [Pause.] Notice where the two sides meet. The energies of the two sides may repel each other along this line, or one side may be reaching or pushing over into the other side. Or the two sides may already be starting to blend and merge.

In a moment, the energies on the two sides of your body will be merging into a single energy. As your intuition guides the process, be open to your innermost truths. A creative resolution will occur between the two sides. First the energies around the fearful side of your body and those around the peaceful side start to mingle and merge. [Pause.] As they blend more completely, a new, unifying energy swirls around your entire being.

Securely surrounded by this unifying energy, the sensations within your body begin to blend into a single energy. A merging of the energies on each side of your body is occurring. Know that this blend is coming about for your highest good. That which is wholesome and valid of the transcendent, peaceful side mixes with the harsher realities from the other side, raising them to a higher level. The two forces synthesize and become a single integrated energy that retains the most important qualities of both. The new mixture will offer peace, wisdom, and strength. The integration between the sides becomes stronger with every breath. You sense newfound hope and understanding. [30-second pause.]

As the new harmonies permeate your body, you may notice that a feeling of resolution and a new direction have become strong in you. As the integration deepens, you may sense a new tranquility about being mortal. Identify the part of your body where the feelings and sensations of serenity and integration are most intense. Find the shape of this part of your body—notice its borders. [Pause.] See its color. [Pause.] Explore its texture. [Pause.] In a moment, you will recognize a symbol that represents a new relationship with death emerging out of these shapes and colors.

Watch as the symbol appears. [Pause.] You may actually see the symbol take form, or you may simply sense what it is. It will further evolve over the next few moments. Relax as it becomes increasingly clear. [20-second pause.]

As a symbol that represents your new relationship with death emerges, prepare to draw it on your shield. [Pause.] Take several deep breaths and begin to stretch your body. [20-second pause.] Open your eyes and draw the symbol on the portion of your shield that is labeled "A Renewed Mythology About Death." As you draw this symbol, you may find that it is changing even as you are creating it or that you have more than one image to draw. Draw whatever comes. When you have completed your drawing, you will find that you have returned to full waking consciousness, feeling refreshed, confident, and able to effectively and creatively meet the requirements of your day.

In your journal, describe your experience with the trance dance and with your body metaphor of resolution. Reflect on the meaning of the new symbol or symbols you drew on your shield. Additionally, consider using the creative projection technique for further examining its personal significance. "Become" the symbol, as you did earlier, and describe yourself as that symbol using first-person present tense. With this ritual, you will have completed the symbolism for each section of your death shield. Add any borders or decorations that will make it more complete for you—people have affixed items ranging from feathers, pine cones, and crystals to heirlooms and photographs. Keep your death shield where you will see it regularly. It will help sustain your awareness of the transformative inner work you have been doing regarding your relationship with death. It also provides a touchstone that can offer emotional protection when you are troubled by existential questions regarding your mortality and your place in the universe. Find confidence and solace in knowing you have taken the journey it records. Meditate on its symbols. They were generated from deep in your psyche, and are a channel to your innermost wisdom. Add new symbols as your relationship with your mortality continues to evolve.

Peg's Symbol

The symbol for Peg's renewed mythology about death was a pair of spawning salmon. "Having lived out their lives, in their last acts they deposit roe and milt on the gravel bar where they were spawned a lifetime before. Their last movements ensure the future of their kind. A cycle is completed, and life ongoing is assured. There is power and renewal in death: dignity and completion. Their uninhabited bodies feed crawdads, snails, bear, 'coons, birds, and bacteria. Nothing is wasted."

Using the creative projection technique, she wrote, "I am a female salmon, symbol of great wisdom in Celtic tradition. I have survived profound hazards, have been hunted for my flesh, have known the depths of the sea. I was born in sweet water, matured in salty, and return to my origins at death. My return has been arduous, as I was drawn upstream over sharp rocks, surmounted cascading waterfalls, and eluded cunning fishermen, swooping eagles, and clawing bears. I know the terrors of low water and the power-sucking force of sudden runoffs from winter rains. I've suffocated in the silt of eroding banks, and I've seen the full moon shine on the river at flood. I persisted, drawn by destiny and delight, for despite its hardships, life has been good. I've known my freedom and my power. I leave a legacy of full living to my offspring."

Robert's Symbol

"My left side represented my fear of death. I saw my strong and healthy left arm begin to wither. It became old, pallid, atrophied. On the other side was pure light—some of the light was from Dawn's twenty-five birthday candles, shining through nearly two decades. When the two energies merged, I had in an instant an astoundingly complex and informative vision. I saw the progression of evolution from the past into the future. It was as though all God's creatures were in an endless line and on a long journey. The line began with reptiles emerging from the ocean. Every species of the animal kingdom was represented. Each creature was a bit further along on the path of evolution than the one before it. I realized that each step forward represented a greater capacity for intelligence and, after a certain point in the line, for compassion as well. The mammals led up to the place where humans began. First were cavemen with clubs. Very close behind me were the early Greeks and Romans.

"The procession also extended ahead of me—as far as I could see into the future. From my place in line—in the present—I could see that off in the future would be people who have evolved much further than we have. I sensed the difference. They emanated a strong, spiritual light in their compassion, serenity, and understanding of the interconnection of all beings. They inspired peace and cooperation. Believing we are evolving toward becoming more like them did not erase the horror of the atrophied arm and oncoming death, but seeing what was up ahead showed a way to become and offered comfort in the rightness of things.

"Being part of this chain gives meaning to life that the fact of personal death cannot erase. The suffering I see along the chain is still beyond my comprehension, but the entire vision at least allows me to place that suffering into a context that gives it some meaning. Also, surprisingly, I found relief in seeing myself as a mere building block—no more than a link in the chain of evolution. I sensed at a deeper level that it is not necessary to be the finished product. My 'perfectionism demons' lose some of their grip with that realization, and I can appreciate who I am rather than dwell on all I am not."

THE FOURTH STAGE:
Toward a Renewed Mythology About Death

As we mature, the psyche continually examines and updates our deepest beliefs and attitudes about death. As you are discovering in this program, one may participate more or less consciously in this natural evolution. In this stage of the program, you will be incorporating all of the work you have done until this point into articulating a more empowering mythology about death.

There is a fundamental paradox about personal myths. Though we need the myths that guide us, we are also required, if we are to stay vital, to perceive the world afresh, to set aside preconceived models and engage fully with what *is*. Such engagement produces moments of clarity in which we may receive new insight about how to meet a particular situation or how we may need to revise a particular guiding myth. On the one hand, it is natural and necessary to create guiding myths so that we are able to give order to our experiences, develop strategies for meeting life, and avoid repeating past errors. On the other hand, it is hazardous to hold on too tightly to our hard-earned insights, rules of behavior, and ways of perceiving. However pertinent our myths may be, clinging to them can cause us to miss those gifted moments when we are able to see with fresh eyes.

Stephen Levine explains that it is our desires and our fears—our models of what we want and what we do not want—that create the greatest emotional suffering. He suggests that if we are able to set aside our inner models and directly contact the truth of the moment, we encounter our "original nature." The experience is purifying and provides a healing lens that "focuses on the potentialities of the moment."[1] He extends these recommendations to the acid test of encountering physical pain. He teaches people the value of meeting even their physical pain with direct awareness—breath full, tightness released, heart and mind open.

It is this attitude of directly meeting your inner experience—not unlike the meditation practices that are our legacy from antiquity—that we hope you will adopt as you complete this program for renewing your mythology about death. Accept with an open heart even your fears, confusion, and unfulfilled longings. It will always serve you to mindfully examine your mythology as you have been doing—exploring its roots, unearthing the conflicts contained within it, and generally evaluating how it has been serving you. But do not grasp too tightly even the best of that mythology. It is a tool for navigation, and it can serve you well, but it can also interfere with your immediate experience of the voyage. There is a time in every journey for putting the maps aside and calling upon serendipity to lead the way. So even as you are reworking your mythology, maintain an openness to the *process* as well as your focus on the task. We suggest that as you go through the remainder of the program, you frequently repeat the mantra that Stephen Levine teaches for moving beyond fears, desires, and expectations: "Notice breath. Soften belly. Open heart."

You will be introduced here to three more personal rituals. They are designed to help you synthesize your experiences to this point into a truly empowering mythology about death. In the first you will receive a death chant that can give you instant access to your renewed mythology and the comfort and good guidance it has to offer. In the second, you will formulate a vision of your own death. There is power in creating a thought form, and holding a positive vision about death has a self-fulfilling impact. In the third ritual, you will review the philosophy of death you formulated at the beginning of the program and elaborate upon ways it has developed and deepened.

PERSONAL RITUAL 13: RECEIVING YOUR DEATH CHANT

In many religious traditions, death is seen as the critical moment in the transformation from life in this world to an existence on more hallowed ground. The thoughts one holds when taking the final breath are often accorded great importance. Lifelong training and preparation may be dedicated to ensure that one will die with the name of God on one's lips, thus returning to the Source already filled with God's presence. When Mahatma Gandhi was struck by an assassin's bullet, he uttered the name Ram, one of the appellations for God, as he fell.[2] Millennia of Jewish people have died with the words "Sh'ma Yisrael, Adonai Elohaynu, Adonai ehkhad" ("Hear, O Israel, the Eternal is our God, the Eternal—'that which always was and always will be'—is One") on their lips.

Levine describes "an extraordinary technique" some Native American tribes devised to prepare for death. Young warriors received— from a grandfather, a dream, a meditation, or a vision quest—a death chant to use throughout their lives to maintain contact with the Great Spirit in times of threat or fear or when in need of healing. The death chant was "an instant centering technique to keep the heart open and the mind clear even in great adversity."[3] Upon falling from a horse, on being attacked by a wild animal, or when burning with fever, the death chant was a constant companion. "Imagine," Levine suggests, "after having sung your death chant perhaps a hundred times in various close calls, when one day you find yourself immobile in the shade of a great boulder, your body burning with snake venom and no one there to help you as the poison begins to paralyze your limbs. But you are not helpless. You've got a powerful channel, a path you can follow, each moment unto death."[4] The death chant created familiarity with the unknown and ushered a serene entry into the world of the spirit. For a person who had made this practice for integrating living and dying a part of life, death could be met with greater peace and clarity, as when one has prepared well for a challenging journey.

Both your death shield and the death chant you are about to receive can be companions that give comfort during difficult times. With practice, your death chant can become a vehicle to transport you to the inspiration of the best of the mythology you have been developing about death and into the open space that is beyond it, where your perceptions are clear and your contact with reality is more direct. It provides a form for imbuing your life with greater clarity and deeper understanding. Consider using it whenever you face threat, loss, or a need for healing.

You will be returning to the "maximum sense of integration" you experienced in the previous ritual and associating that experience with your death chant. In this ritual, your death chant will actually emerge out of this "maximum sense of integration" and the feelings of peace and understanding that are part of it. You may need to repeat the previous ritual a number of times before you are satisfied with the degree of peace and integration it offers. The following instructions will take you through a modified form of that ritual and lead you to your death chant.

Recall the trance dance you used to open the space for a new level of integration in your mythology regarding death. You will begin here with a similar dance, designed to open—in body, heart, and mind—space to receive your death chant. Select music that is the same as or similar to that which you used for your trance dance. Move to the music with an awareness that you are inviting your deeper self to devise a death chant, words or patterned sound you can invoke to draw solace and healing. Move rapidly and emphatically to the beat. Continue until your body is tired and your mind is clear. Finally, stop the music and find a spot where you can lie down as you prepare to receive your death chant.

Your body is already becoming calm as you focus your mind on these instructions. Bring your attention to your breathing. [Pause.] Listen for and feel each in breath and each out breath. [Pause.] Notice how your stomach and chest fill . . . and empty. [Pause.] As you continue to breathe and relax, you are better able to concentrate on my voice and on the suggestions I will offer. If outside sounds or passing thoughts cross your mind, they fade quietly into the background just as they occur. Your breathing is slow and deep as you relax more completely with each of your next five breaths. One [pause]; two [pause]; three [pause]; four [pause]; five [pause].

Recall how in the earlier ritual one side of your body represented your primal fear of death. Again, the sensations symbolizing your primal fear of death become vivid. [Pause.] They may include coldness, tightness, heaviness, or darkness. [Pause.] These sensations become particularly vivid in the hand that is on the fearful side of your body.

Recall the sensations you felt in the other, peaceful side of your body. [Pause.] These sensations, symbolizing tranquility about death, also become vivid. [Pause.] They may include warmth, light, or tingling. [Pause.] These sensations become particularly vivid in the hand that is on this peaceful side of your body.

Recall how the sensations in the two sides of your body blended into a single unified energy. [Pause.] This time, the blending can begin in your hands. Raise your hands, palms facing, about two feet apart. Explore the sensations in the hand that represents your fear of death. [Pause.] Shift your attention to the sensations in the hand that represents a sense of peace about death. Just as opposites attract, there is a force that is drawing your hands together.

Slowly, your hands will come together. The instant they touch, you will feel a merging of the energies between the two sides of your body. A single, unified creative integration of these two energies will encompass your hands, permeate your body, and leave you with a deepened inner harmony. [Pause.] Hands coming together now. [Pause.] When your hands meet, your fingers may intertwine. [Pause.] The two energies are now synthesizing, integrating, becoming a single energy, retaining the best qualities of both. Feel them merging with every breath. [30-second pause.]

As the newly integrated energies permeate your hands and body, you have stronger and stronger feelings of resolution and of new direction. Lowering your hands, the energy flows between the two sides of your body, and the sensations merge into a single unified feeling. [Pause.] Identify the part of your body where this feeling of integration is most

*intense. [Pause.] Begin to breathe into this feeling. Your breathing is slow
and deep.*

*Allow your breath to pass over your vocal cords with each exhalation
so a sound results. [Pause.] Allow the sound to develop in such a manner that it expresses a harmony between the two sides of your body, a constructive integration of primal fears and serenity. [20-second pause.]
Experiment aloud with this sound. Play with it until the sound becomes
a chant or a song. The chant will express this feeling of integration, along
with whatever peace and understanding you have come to about the nature of life and death. The chant may be made of words that you recognize or sounds you do not recognize. It will involve you physically,
emotionally, and spiritually. Receive your death chant now and allow it
to develop. Repeat it until you come into a deep sense of peace and inner
harmony.*

You may recreate this space any time you wish by taking three
deep breaths, bringing your hands together as you recall the feeling
of integration, and squeezing them as you repeat your death chant.
Do this now. Take three deep breaths. As you recite your death
chant, bring your hands together and squeeze them. Continue chanting as a feeling of integration and wholeness moves through your
body. Repeat this practice frequently over the next few weeks, until
your death chant is able to take you reliably into the tranquility,
openness, and understanding that are inspired by your renewed
mythology about death. Like the Native American warrior, you may
invoke your death chant in times of threat, fear, sorrow, pain, or need
for connection with the Great Spirit.

Peg's Death Chant

"Though characteristically I wanted to be thoroughly 'original,'
the theme of my death chant is very familiar:

> This is a good day to die.
> The Sun will rise tomorrow.

This is a good day to die.
The River flows endlessly.
This is a good day to die.
I follow my bliss into the Earth."

Death chants are highly personal, and Peg's chant has different meaning for her than the same words might have for another person. Asking her to elaborate on the personal significance of her death chant, she equated "this is a good day to die" with "I have no regrets, no unfinished business; I am not afraid." In affirming to herself daily, and in proclaiming to the universe, that she *is* prepared to die, she is also reminding herself that because life is part of a larger cycle, she can proceed with a looser grip on her attachments to the earthly world. With the middle lines, Peg affirms her belief that "there is no ending." The "waters of life flow endlessly and inexhaustibly." The final line, "I follow my bliss into the Earth," offers Peg a pleasing and comforting image: "I complete my cycle, release my spirit, recycle my chemicals."

Robert's Death Chant

"I started with a deep, solid resonant sound that came up from my toes and seemed to vibrate every cell of my body. It brought about a warmth that enveloped me in a unified, pulsating feeling. It was very pleasurable. Then I sensed that some part of me wanted to speak. I sensed that I should keep making the sound, more quietly now, and allow it to form into words. I had an image that I was handing over the controls to this part deep inside. The first words that sort of tumbled out, and in a rather pleasing melody, were these:

Come listen to my song for you.
Come listen to my song for you.
Come hear your death chant.
Come hear your death chant.

"The words certainly got my attention. I listened inwardly. There was a silence for a long time. Then I began to glimpse or hear—I'm not sure which—another verse. Soon it was coming through, in a similar melody.

> You who do not feel ready to die.
> You who do not feel ready to die.
> Come hear your death chant.
> Come hear your death chant.

"I kept listening, and new verses kept coming:

> Death like life is real.
> Death like life is real.
> Death like time is false.
> Death like time is false.
>
> You must stop to see
> What's been always there.
> You must stop to see
> What's been always there.
>
> So you know the timeless
> As you live your life.
> So you know the timeless
> As you live your life.
>
> You must stop to see
> What's been always there.
> So you know the timeless
> As you live your life.
>
> From your depths
> You find
> The timeless space
> That transcends death [repeated perhaps a
>   dozen times].

"This last verse is the part I take with me as my death chant. It is a reminder for me that death is there to be reckoned with, however much I keep it out of my mind. It is a fact of life. It is also a reminder that the 'timeless space' that reveals the nature of death and shows me that death is not the end is always within me. The primary effect as I'm deepening my understanding of death is that I am getting internal agitation and support, perhaps I could call it inspiration, to more frequently find the 'timeless space' that exists in my depths and to live from it as fully as I am able."

PERSONAL RITUAL 14: PERSONAL DEATH FABLE, "A VISION OF A GOOD DEATH"

Recall the death fables you wrote earlier: "Death in the Shadow of Fear" and "Death in the Light of Transcendence." For this ritual, you will write a third story. It will reflect an integration between your primal death anxiety and whatever sense of serenity you have achieved regarding your awareness of death. This story, however, rather than featuring the character from the first two fables, will be about you and an event that might be in your future. In this personal death fable, you will generate for yourself a vision of a good death. In that vision, you will have come to terms with your fears, and you will have been successful in finding an inner sense of peace about your eventual departure from this world.

William Irwin Thompson describes the relationship between our inner images and the life we live: "Like a lure-casting fisherman, man seems to cast a fantasy far in front of him and then slowly reel himself into it."[5] Our inner images and thought forms hold a magnetic charge—they draw us toward performing the very actions that will bring them into being. Your life imitates your personal mythology as much as the other way around. Desirable changes begin to occur when you transform your mythology, making it more constructive, more supportive of your highest potential, and more attuned to your deepest wisdom.

If your life's journey is organized around a vision of declining health, diminishing pleasure, fading opportunities, and a dreadful ending, your path into the future will seem different and *be* different than if your guiding vision about aging can offer hope and highlight opportunities. Some people hold a vision of themselves in old age as enjoying a time of increased wisdom, as being able to slow down and bask in the simpler pleasures of life, as taking satisfaction in past achievements, and as savoring the relief of no longer being responsible for making the social wheel spin around. Though such visions do not ensure one's fate, they inspire choices that maximize the chances that the vision will become reality. Sometimes a vision will occur spontaneously. Consider the following experience, which was reported by a fifty-six-year-old woman:[6]

> Traveling in northern California, alone, on my birthday, filled with reverence and awe after hiking through a redwood grove, I had a vision of my own death. While I am lying facedown on the cool fragrant humus of needles and ferns, a shaft of light penetrates the indescribably sacred grove and falls on me. There is a dark square of redwood forest with four guardian trees at the cardinal points. I envision a grave hollowed out among the roots without disturbing them. The roots form an angular cradle. Three men and a woman carry me toward the cavity. One man is my husband, tender, thin, and old. Another is a beloved friend. The third's face is an unrecognizable shadow. The woman is a lovely young stranger.
>
> I know that I am ninety-four. My hair is downy white, and my face is brown and wrinkled, like a friendly walnut. My eyes are alert and unafraid. I am dressed in a loose, nondescript gown, and I have a lemon-yellow scarf around my neck. All my fleshiness used up, my body is light and nearly transparent. There is little of substance left of who I was. They lay me in the cradle of roots, and we smile, one at a time, at each other. It is

clear there is no anguish here. I rest on my earthly cradle and look up at the splendid trunks of the trees. I smell the pungent dampness. My breath leaves my body for the last time. A squirrel runs out on a limb, excitedly, and drops a cone into my bed.

This woman later wrote about the place that this vision came to have in her life:

It is not clear to me how much of this mythic revelation is made from fragments of dreams, wish fulfillment, denial, or sacred vision and timewarp. I no longer care. Having been granted such a gratifying hallucination, delusion, holy intuition, or reverie, I find it wisest to believe. I choose, as an educated woman, to keep that myth out in front of me. Because I believe that I will die as envisioned in the forest, I greatly enhance my opportunity to have a good death. Even if I am wrong, I am making my present infinitely more tolerable. If I start thinking of myself as a charred body in Armageddon, I am certainly destroying my present, and I may be contributing to making it happen—nothing productive comes from it; there is no good in it. If people didn't get any more rarefied than that, than to give themselves a vision of a good death, that could affect all kind of things: what you eat, the kinds of stress you put yourself under, all the things you have to do to give yourself a good death.

By using your imagination to fashion a plausible death scenario, you will have an opportunity to create a positive and constructive vision about your own death. You will also, in your imagination, be able to experience how your death chant might provide you with comfort and strength in your final hour. First read about Peg's and Robert's death scenes. Then find surroundings that evoke inspiration and peace, perhaps a place with great natural beauty. Place the heading

"My Personal Death Fable" on a fresh page of your journal. Take time to relax. Tune inwardly to a deeper voice. Imagine the setting of your final hour, note your age, recognize how you look and feel, and be aware of who else is with you. You are seeking a vision that you will *want* to "cast far in front" of yourself, a vision you can "reel" yourself into with the daily choices that shape your life.

Peg's Personal Death Fable

"I am very old. I am used up, not broken or diseased. My body is used up like a fallen fir log, nurse to ferns and a thousand life forms, dissolving formlessly into Earth.

"I have used up my ambition, ego, foolishness. What is left is love without boundaries and experience. The belly and breast scars of my childbearing, my forehead lined by countless frowns of anger and puzzlement, my mouth's brackets shaped by ten thousand laughs, my bony feet, veterans of many the long mile walked, are fading snapshots of my living.

"Today is my death day. Long years of wonderment watching the forest's seasons have removed my fear. There is only longing. It is midspring, perhaps my birthday, and the daffodils are nodding enthusiastically under the alder trees. I sit among them, my palms touching the earth, my back pressed against the moss-clothed bark of a great maple's trunk.

"Before me is the shining creek, turning sinuous curves through reeds. I feel the salmon's call to give life even as I die. My body will melt but be no more wasted than the fir log. Beside me is my husband, old now, too. We are the only two human forms here on the banks of the Yaquina, but we are not alone—the spirits of the land attend us. I raise my eyes to his a last time; our life has been long and good. He will miss me, but he will find his way. We know each other's thoughts.

"I think of my parents and forgive them their humanity as I forgive my own. It is a good day to die. I rest my head a last time on my husband's chest, feel his long arm snug me close. One tear falls for words of love left unspoken in my life. The sun catches the falling tear, lights a star within, and I am part of it all—again."

Robert's Personal Death Fable

"I'm at home. For the last time I inspect each of the sacred objects that adorn my room. Each holds fond memories, pleases the eye, and offers inspiration. I tell my children and my grandchildren what every item means to me. And I tell them what each of them means to me, each as unique and special as the sacred objects that surround us. They each have some parting words for me. They tell me some of their memories of times we've spent together, and they tell of qualities in myself that they value and will remember. I say good-bye to each of them. Also, two of my closest friends are there to say good-bye. One of them tells me that 'good-bye' means 'God be with ye.' We are in deep peace with one another.

"I know my time is very near, and I ask to be alone with Dawn. We have been preparing for this moment over the past few weeks. We conduct a ceremony with candles and pictures and talk about the best parts of the life we've shared together. I begin to sing my death chant, feeling its solid, resonant tone welling up from deep within me:

> From your depths
> You find
> The timeless space
> That transcends death.

"Although I am weak, the effect is profound. Like so many times before, my death chant brings me into my 'timeless space.' Dawn begins to sing her death chant in harmony with mine. Our eyes meet. The sounds merge into one, and our spirits seem to join as well. Time stops as we come into communion with each other and with the forces of life and death. From this holy union, we say a final good-bye. I close my eyes as I softly continue my death chant. A tranquility comes upon me. I am complete and content. I drift peacefully out of my body and into the light."

PERSONAL RITUAL 15: YOUR PHILOSOPHY OF DEATH REVISITED

"Let death be thy teacher," advised Saint Augustine. Your philosophy of death codifies what you have learned from death's counsel. At the beginning of this program, you described your philosophy of death. Here you will describe new developments in that philosophy. First enact another round of the dialogue between the characters representing your fear of death and your resources for transcending that fear. Unrehearsed, continue for at least ten more minutes. Explore whether the work to this point has made it possible for the two characters to achieve a better mutual understanding and an ability to support each other's concerns. Summarize such progress in your journal. Then review the symbols on your death shield and reread what you wrote earlier in your journal under the heading "My Philosophy of Death." Place the heading "My Philosophy of Death Revisited" at the top of a new page. Write freely for at least ten minutes, focusing on areas where your philosophy of death may be progressing from what you wrote earlier.

From Peg's "Philosophy of Death Revisited"

"I can bring back my fear by conjuring ugly images. I can make cases for uncertainty. But if life has taught me one thing, it's the awareness that it is better to feel good than to feel rotten. I believe all creation is energy—things, space, and forces—all are energy. Physics teaches us that energy is neither created nor destroyed but that it frequently changes form. Nothing is wasted. I prefer the poetry of 'spirit' to the mechanistic sound of 'energy.'

"I believe that there is more to me than the body I gratefully occupy. This *something* includes and transcends my consciousness and personality. How spirit came into being and what (if anything) is its destination are questions too difficult for me: I cannot know the face of God. I can only recognize that the orchestration of the cosmos and the cells of my body are purposeful. Because I have the capacity to feel union with the creations that make up the Earth, and because feeling good is better than feeling terrorized, I choose to invest my energy in the ways that feel holy (whole) to me.

"My life task lies in knowing and directing the spirit that is *me*. I do not believe I exist or can function without relation to the energies around me—environmental, human, and spiritual. Therefore, it follows that I will direct myself toward the goal of harmony. No simple task for a rebel, a pragmatist, and a coward. I must become a healer, a mystic, and a heroine if I am to have a good death."

From Robert's "Philosophy of Death Revisited"

Robert discussed some of the changes in his beliefs and attitude that occurred while he was going through the program. For one, he had begun to read extensively the teachings of the various great religions regarding afterlife. He reflected, "I'm less sure now than ever that the life hereafter is a heavenly shift into uninterrupted peace and joy, as I'd previously imagined. But I feel more sure that there *is* a life hereafter and that there is some plan, some Intelligence larger than anything I can imagine running the show."

Robert also reflected on the difference between people who have good deaths and those who do not. "Those who do their part to have a good death have learned some important things about living. They have learned how to be in the moment and to face whatever is there with, as the program advises, an open heart and an open mind. They are able to work through and let go of past disappointments, to not live in their expectations for the future, to just be in the eternal present. I don't know why it is so hard to just slow down and 'be here now.' But somehow it seems to have a lot to do with whether I will ever make peace with my mortality."

Another topic Robert addressed concerned the contribution his life would make to the world. "I once believed that all the world's problems would be solved by technological advances, and I had a religious fervor for my work helping design [architecturally] the world in which we would live. Now that technology emerges as much the villain as the savior, my work doesn't provide meaning for me the way it once did. I keep coming to the realization that if I am to help the world, there is truth to the old cliche about starting with oneself. Developing more compassion, love, and serenity within myself is my best bet."

THE FIFTH STAGE:
Bringing Your Renewed Mythology About Death into Life

You have now completed the major portion of this program for cultivating a more empowering mythology for confronting death. The program was designed to show you how to actively participate, within the light of conscious awareness, in the stages through which we believe one's death mythology naturally evolves. In working with the personal myths of several thousand people, we have learned that by mindfully walking through the five-stage process you are about to complete, people come to understand the deeper mythic forces acting upon them. They also grow to be more capable of influencing these forces and of living in a positive relationship with them.

Each of the five stages has a specific purpose and corresponds with one of the phases by which personal myths seem to naturally develop. In the preliminary work, you gained an overview of your mythology regarding your mortality by writing your philosophy of death, journeying back in time to some of your earliest memories about death, and creating a death shield to symbolize and keep track of the discoveries the program offered about your relationship with death.

Having established this background, you entered the first stage of the program, which was organized around the theme "Rattling Your System of Death Denial." Much of the difficulty people have regarding death is closely related to repressed or unconscious fears. In this part of the program, you excavated this anxiety, using personal rituals designed to "open your heart to your deeper fears," to take your awareness to the historical "foundation" of some of these fears, and to create a death fable called "Death in the Shadow of Fear."

In the second stage of the program, "Transcending the Fear of Death," you searched for counterforces to your fear of death, and you focused particularly on your psyche's quest to find ways of transcending death, such as in attempts to achieve symbolic immortality. You closed your work in this stage with a second death fable that was the polar opposite of the first: "Death in the Light of Transcendence."

In the third stage, you attempted to bring resolution to the natural conflict between the fear of death and images of transcending death. You conducted an inner dialogue between your fear of death and prospects for transcending death, opened an internal space for a new and deeper resolution of this conflict, and established a body metaphor of this resolution.

In the fourth stage, your renewed mythology, reflecting the resolution of inner conflict that was the focus of the previous stage, was further articulated, expanded, and anchored in your psyche. Opening to receive your death chant, creating a personal death fable, and expanding your philosophy of death all served these ends. In this, the fifth stage, the task is to weave your renewed mythology into your life. It involves stepping out into the practical world and making changes at that level. It is composed of three personal rituals: "Attending to That Which Will Survive You," "Creation of a Ceremony for the Final Hour and Beyond," and "A 'Right Relationship' with What You Do Between Now and Your Final Hour."

PERSONAL RITUAL 16: ATTENDING TO THAT
WHICH WILL SURVIVE YOU

Religious and spiritual systems often teach that to live in peace about death requires that one be ready in an instant to let go of life in the physical world. Ritual preparation for death to come at any moment can be found in many traditions. The ancient warrior went into battle fully prepared to meet death. Recall the lines beginning "If I should die before I wake . . ." from the familiar bedtime prayer. Among some Orthodox Jewish groups, prayers designed to be recited before death are also voiced each night before going to sleep. There is, for instance, a nightly liturgy for forgiving anyone to whom your heart is closed, though they have committed a transgression against you, and another to confess your own transgressions and ask forgiveness. Thus, each evening, one performs a ritual of purification and is ready for death if it comes in the night.[1] Through such practices, not only does one have an opportunity to cherish what one loves and to make peace with what is difficult, but also, each night before entering the "little death" of sleep, one becomes a bit more prepared for the final passing. Sleep becomes a training ground for dying.

Putting your worldly affairs in order is another way of preparing for death. As you move through the following ritual, you will be considering a number of steps that can be taken in order to live with greater preparedness for the inevitable last hour. If you have not taken these steps, we strongly suggest that you do. Simply attending to these matters and making the decisions they require can serve as a rite of passage, leading to greater peace and acceptance about the eventuality of death. If you have already dealt with these items, we suggest that you rethink the decisions you have made from the perspective of your renewed mythology about death.

In either case, address the following topics in your journal. Give yourself some space before going from one topic to the next. Begin your work with each topic by meditating on your death shield and then repeating your death chant, along with any ceremony (such as your trance dance) that might open you to your deepest wisdom as you address each issue. Only then begin to write.

1. With whom do I have unfinished business that I want laid to rest while I am still alive? Regarding each person you identify, create a plan that specifies what you will do and how and when you will do it.

2. Are there letters or poems or other forms of communication I want specific people to receive after I die? What arrangements must I make for this?

3. What would I like done with my best works (art, writing, creations related to my profession, etc.)? How will I make these intentions known?

4. What are my desires regarding burial or cremation? Would I like to have any of my body parts donated for transplant or medical research? How will I make these intentions known?

5. What would I like to leave others? If I do not have a will, how can I go about writing one that is in proper legal form?

Other issues may also come to mind—from checking that your life insurance is in order, to making arrangements so that extraordinary measures will not be taken to prolong your life if you are in a coma with no reasonable expectation for survival, to making peace with yourself about a transgression you committed three decades ago. Add other topics as you are moved to do so.[2] Begin your work on each topic by bringing yourself into a clear and peaceful internal space, using the kinds of activities suggested above. Appreciate even the process of entering this space. Though it may have consisted primarily of internal activities, think of entering the space as itself a creative ritual. This puts your intention here into a proper perspective and brings you into a state of receptivity more likely to evoke your highest wisdom for the tasks at hand.

Peg's Reflections

1. I have unfinished business with very few who are still alive. I want to release my anger (and righteousness) at several people, even though I take some sort of perverse satisfaction in rejecting them. My plan is to rechannel my energy. When I think, "Greg is a brutal, selfish man," I will repeat until I believe it, "Greg's essence is good." Hard.

2. I want my children, particularly, to listen to me read *Blind Raftery: Seven Nights of a Wake*. I've made tapes before and sent them, but as far as I know they haven't taken time to hear me. I will

make new, better recordings. Wrap them nicely, put them with my things to be found after my death. I'll enclose a personal, private note to each. I want a few others to have copies. I'll see to it.

3. My best works are walking around laughing and living; they are beyond and free of my "intentions."

4. Regarding burial, wrap me in unbleached cotton cloth and put me in moist ground on The Land. Put me deep, where the taproot of a redwood can be nourished with the minerals of my body, so that when a great grandchild looks up a massive trunk, he can think, "This place feels familiar, and it feels safe."

5. I will make a list of what to do with my "things" and entrust the list to my husband.

Robert's Reflections

1. My own death feels so far off in the future that it was hard to get into this assignment. Then I thought about my parents, whom I expect to outlive. My parents are well along in years. Although they still enjoy good health, they decline noticeably between our annual visits. I have sat in judgment of what I consider to be their inflexible and outdated values during these obligatory visits, occasionally allowing a contemptuous remark to slip out. I've never quite accepted them for not taking what I consider the higher road in the second half of their lives. I've been unwilling to forgive them for not letting go of attitudes and securities that have been their companions for a lifetime. Right now that looks really dumb on my part. They gave me the best they had. They are about to leave forever, and I sit around allowing my judgments to put a wedge between us! They may irritate me, but I do love them, I will miss them deeply, and I want them to feel my deepest love and appreciation for all they've given me while they are still here. The visit next month will be very different.

2. I've always thought I'd like to write something toward the end of my life, a kind of "Important Things About Life from the

Vantage Point of One of Your Ancestors," to be passed down through the generations. I'm forty-two. This is probably at least the halfway mark. I wanted that essay for future generations to contain my wisest, so it has always been something I'd do sometime off in the distant future. But maybe I'm ready to begin the first draft. I could put it on the word processor and revise it annually. That would help track any advances in wisdom from one year to the next, and it would keep me attuned to promoting such advances. It also gives me something constructive to do with my awareness of my mortality.

3. Oh, God, here we go again with an assignment that calls for preparation as if death is just around the corner. Okay, it could be! I'll pull together a little scrapbook of the highlights of my life. I'll include photographs, mementos, news clippings, and little narratives. I'll find three or four of the best letters I've ever received. I'll include copies of a few of the best letters I've ever written. I will give it to Bobby [his first child] for his next birthday to keep as a legacy for future generations. Maybe each year I'll use the week of his birthday to add anything new to it and also to update my "Important Things About Life" statement.

4. I remember discussions with my father about the way cremation helps free the soul of earthly attachments. Seems sort of farfetched right now, but nonetheless, I've thought of cremation as the proper way to dispose of a body ever since. But now that I'm always looking for the "natural way" to do things, the idea of being laid to rest in the ground, with no coffin separating me from the earth, seems more natural. I'm not sure. Cremation still offers an image of being released that is more appealing than rotting in the ground. I guess it's time to make a decision about burial or cremation. I'll discuss it with Dawn. Whether it's cremation or burial, I think I'd like them to wait about three days so there is plenty of time for the life energies to peaceably leave my body—as in the Kirlian photographs where you see how the energy of a leaf fades each hour after it's been

picked. I've also been very ambivalent about donating my body parts. It's a little silly, because I'll be somewhere else, but I feel unsettled when I think of various parts haphazardly dispersed. What came to me as I was reflecting on it this morning is that I'd feel good knowing that one of my organs, whatever is needed most, would be available for transplant.

5. No question here. Dawn and then the kids get everything. And I pray that the way we're steering this planet will take a sharp turn for the better so that Bobby and Jill can make good use of my hard-earned assets for a long, long time.

PERSONAL RITUAL 17: CREATION OF A CEREMONY
FOR THE FINAL HOUR AND BEYOND

For this ritual, you will go on a guided imagery journey in which you create a fantasy about your final hour, your funeral or memorial service, and your eulogy. First reread your personal death fable. The vision of your final hour will be similar to the one in your death fable, but this time, in addition to experiencing it in deep fantasy, you are to focus on the kind of ceremony or ritual you would like to have occur. These visions of your final hour, service, and eulogy will be created while you are in "sacred time."

The following guided imagery instructions begin in the same manner as the earlier ritual, "A View of 'Symbolic Immortality' Through Sacred Time." Again, bring yourself into a mood that is conducive to entering sacred time before you perform the ritual. Your trance dance, death chant, or an approach you devised in a previous ritual may help bring you to such a space. When you are ready to start, find a comfortable position, take a deep breath, and close your eyes.

The path you will be following into sacred time is marked by physical relaxation and uplifting memories. Settle in comfortably—finding an inner quiet, peace, and warmth. [Pause.] Thank your body for its hard work and good service. [Pause.] Find the parts of your body that need special attention, healing, or rest. Picture a warm, wise hand filled with a fragrant ointment gently touching and appreciating those parts. Focus your attention and sense the melting, calming relaxation that comes into those sore and tired places. [30-second pause.]

As you focus on my voice, other sounds fade away. All is well with you for this journey into sacred time. You are always free to return to ordinary consciousness by simply opening your eyes and exhaling fully, and you are just as free to explore the riches of your inner world. You will recall all you need of this experience, and you will emerge from it with insight and power. You can move and adjust yourself at any time, yawning and stretching, rearranging until your body is peaceful and satisfied.

Begin to reflect on the holiest, most sacred times of your past. [Pause.] Remember a moment of shared love. [Pause.] Recall seeing a newborn child. [Pause.] You have felt yourself awed by a sunset, a waterfall, or the seashore. [Pause.] You have heard inspiring music [pause]; seen great art [pause]; savored a creative breakthrough [pause]; sat in an awe-inspiring cathedral or other place of reverence. [Pause.] Focus on a time that was particularly inspiring. [Pause.] Recall it vividly. [Pause.] Relive it in each of your senses. Breathe into the vision [pause], the sounds [pause], the feelings [pause]. Let go into the memory. [20-second pause.] Soon you will hear counting, from one to seven. When you hear the number seven, you will be fully relaxed and deep in sacred time.

One. As you bask in the inspiring feelings of the scene you have remembered, the healing hand sensitively massages your back, shoulders, and neck. You sigh, content.

Two. The healing hand moves to your face, massaging your forehead, eyes, cheeks, scalp, mouth, and jaw. Each breath fills your awareness. Unhurried, your sense of sacred time deepens.

Three. The muscles and joints of your arms and legs are rejuvenated by the healing hand. You exhale fully, feeling vitally alive and relaxed.

Four. The healing hand finds wounded or weary parts in the trunk of your body, nourishing them with tender touch. Your breathing is deep and pleasurable.

Five. The healing hand continues to touch away your pains as you exhale your tiredness, hurt, and disillusion.

Six. Fully relaxed, you can notice a pleasant tingling on your skin. As you smile, you feel a deep sense of peacefulness.

Seven. Your heart is open. You are absorbed in the comfortable sensations of warmth and heaviness. Your breathing fills the moment. You have entered sacred time. [20-second pause.]

Continuing to breathe deeply, watch your breath rising and falling. [Pause.] Your mind is clear as you savor the heightened awareness of this open moment. [60-second pause.]

From this heightened awareness, your appreciation of life is amplified, along with a sense of peace about death. You can feel yourself, now, moving forward in time. You are moving forward to the occasion of your own death. In this death scenario, precisely the atmosphere you would desire for your last moments on earth already exists. [Pause.] Visualize yourself now in this final hour. [Pause.] As you survey the situation, you can vividly see or sense yourself in the scene, along with any others who are there. People are relating to you and to one another just as you might wish. [Pause.] You are about to imagine a ceremony or ritual to maintain or heighten the mood. It may be performed by you alone or with others. [Pause.] In the following silence, you will experience the entire ceremony. [45-second pause.]

As the moment of death approaches, you begin to recite your death chant. Start to use it now and continue it as you imagine your consciousness moving out of your body. In your imagination, allow your death chant to be the bridge as you leave your body and come into a space from which you will be able to view your funeral or memorial service. Slowly move into that space now. [Pause.] From here in your imagination, you can see your funeral or memorial service. Again, the atmosphere is exactly as you would like it to be.

Survey the scene, noting who is there. [Pause.] Your eulogy is about to be given. Look at the person who is beginning to deliver it. In the following silence, you hear it. [30-second pause.]

From this privileged vantage point, you realize that you will be returning to your body and continuing with your life. [Pause.] Consider how you wish to live differently. [Pause.] What insights from this unique perspective do you intend to bring back with you? [20-second pause.] Now it is time to reenter your body. [Pause.] You return fully to your normal body awareness, noticing your breathing, sensing your weight against that which is supporting you, feeling your hands and feet and neck. [Pause.] You have fully returned to your present age.

Peaceful in your body now, you will soon bring your awareness back into the room. Counting from seven back to one, you will be able to recall all you need of this experience. When you hear the number one, you will be fully awake and aware of the present moment, as if returning from a wonderful nap. Seven, taking a deep breath. [Pause.] Six, moving your toes and feeling the circulation. [Pause.] Five, moving your fingers. [Pause.] Four, stretching your shoulders, neck, and face muscles. [Pause.] Three, breathing deeply, smiling as you return. [Pause.] Two, bringing your attention back to the room. [Pause.] One, opening your eyes, feeling refreshed, confident, and able to effectively and creatively meet the requirements of your day.

In your journal, describe the ceremony or ritual you would like to have as part of your final hour, the nature of the funeral or memorial service you envisioned, the eulogy you heard, and any insights or resolutions you brought back with you. As you complete this section of your journal, be tuned in for the wording of an epitaph. Write an epitaph at the end of your journal entry. If any instructions should be given to your loved ones about plans for your final hour, funeral, memorial service, or epitaph, make plans to convey them. A growing number of people are asking that, following their own deaths, verses be read for them out of modernized adaptations of the *Tibetan Book of the Dead,* such as Sogyal Rinpoche's *The Tibetan Book of Living and Dying*[3] and E. J. Gold's *American Book of the Dead.*[4]

Peg's Death Ceremony

"First, it's a wake. A wake is a time to remember, to feast, to clear the air, and to summarize the lessons of the life lived. I've said my intentions in my book *Blind Raftery:*

> For my wake, you're to gather the neighbors seven nights runnin'. Each night seven songs will be sung in memorium, seven kinds of cakes eaten, seven glasses of the good stuff drunk in toast to my blessed memory, and seven stories told each night that show my character off in a pleasin' light. Seven auld women will keen as though all their sons were going into exile. Seven pipers will flail and abuse the atmosphere with mournful tunes until all present have taken aboard enough of the good stuff to tire of the lamenting and demand a hornpipe or jig. Through it all the fiddlers of the countryside will stand at one side and play the songs that fit the stories, so that all may wonder at the wake of Blind Raftery and remember my doings at least until they're planted themselves. At the end of the seventh night each one present will lay a hand on my fiddle, listenin' the whole time with heads cocked to one side. I'll play a tune from heaven—or wherever I find myself—that will bring a blessing of a peculiar nature to them as hears.

"It is fine with me for details to be changed to fit the circumstances, but decorum will *not* be maintained, pleasure will be had, and harmony promoted. I want my children—now grown and separated—to love and see the good in one another.

"Plant me deep in the earth on The Land. Put redwoods at the cardinal points, not more than thirty feet from where I'm dissolving. I'd like ferns, spring bulbs in plenty, lilacs, and my loved ones' favorite plants 'round about. I'd like a stone lintel made like the dolmens of Ireland erected and hung with bells, wind chimes, prisms, bright ribbons, swinging pots for burning sage and lavender, and other objects of beauty and ceremony. I'd like a little shelter, a gazebo or such, set close by. It should be suitable for sleeping, lovemaking, or quiet times of contemplation in all weather. A winding path, with comfortable seats in pleasant bowers, suits me well. There should be no fence, but a hedge of fruiting plants to feed the birds and deer is desirable."

This was Peg's epitaph:

> Hear me in the wind.
> Feel me in the river.
> Touch me in the ferns.
> Taste me in the blackberries.
> See me in the season's change.
> Be glad in the moment
> And remember me with smiles.

Robert's Death Ceremony

"First I saw the ceremony with Dawn that I described in my personal death fable, except we were outdoors on a sunny day. She was wearing a flowing purple velvet gown. I was in loose white clothing, lying on a mat surrounded by grass and trees. The most powerful part of the vision was when we were singing our death chants in harmony, eyes and hearts locked together. I knew our hearts would remain connected long after our eyes had separated.

"Again, it was hard to envision my memorial service because I think so much is supposed to happen between now and then. But I forced myself to imagine a memorial. It is a warm day on the Oregon coast. The spot I envision is within two hours from our home. I have been dead three days, watching from up here with compassion and love as various people react to the news of my death, and now I am ready for today's ceremony because I know it is time to move on. Dawn carries my ashes in a porcelain vase made for us years earlier by a dear friend. She will keep the vase. The ashes are to be buried under a sturdy spruce tree where we've watched bald eagles light on the cliffs overlooking the rugged coastline. A goblet filled from my precious 1974 bottle of Mt. Eden cabernet sauvignon is passed among the twenty-some relatives and close friends who are present. Taking the goblet, each one reminisces about me.

"I find it gratifying that they have such good stories to tell. I am pleased that my friends remember me in terms of my humor, compassion, and intelligence. I experience my love for each of them with a purity that I realize I wish I could have expressed down there on earth. Maybe I still can. I also appreciate the role each has played in my journey. I send blessings from beyond as each drinks of the goblet. It is clear that I will be missed, but it is also clear that I have lived fully and enjoyed my life. Being carved on the spruce tree is a sort of epitaph, adapted from my death chant: 'Behold the timeless space that transcends death!' "

PERSONAL RITUAL 18: A "RIGHT RELATIONSHIP" WITH WHAT
YOU DO BETWEEN NOW AND YOUR FINAL HOUR

You are coming to the close of this program for opening your heart to the fact of death and thus to a richer understanding of the foundations of your life. We believe that such openness and understanding are vital to maintaining a "right relationship" with death. This program has been one pathway for cultivating such a relationship. The process is lifelong. A right relationship with death leads, in turn, to a right relationship with life. From time to time, as you gather new experience and understanding, issues you examined here will return to the forefront of your attention. The techniques you have used can be repeated, and the principles you have learned can be adapted to new areas of concern.

This step-by-step guide, however, has escorted you as far as it can on your journey toward an enhanced relationship with death and thus life. It is time for you to initiate the next steps. In this final ritual, you will commit yourself to take action toward further establishing this "right relationship." Some possibilities may have occurred to you while you were going through the program. There may be a ritual you would like to repeat or a difficult issue that requires further attention. You may decide upon additional steps for making your environment more receptive or your daily routine more supportive of the guidance your new mythology offers. You may need to affirm your intent to protect space for your inner exploration. Sabbaths and other holy days have, in the past, ensured that time was consecrated for attending to one's spiritual life. Our culture, for the most part, no longer supports such traditions, and the responsibility for setting aside the time and space for such inner work falls on each of us.

For this ritual, once again begin with your trance dance and/or your death chant to enter a space from which your deeper spirit will illuminate your understanding. From that space, ask about actions you might take to establish a more fulfilling relationship with life and with death. Quietly listen to the answers that are within you.

When you have returned to your normal waking consciousness, describe in your journal the actions that came to you. Consider the purpose or positive intent of each. Decide if you believe this action is the best way of accomplishing its positive intent. If it is not, envision an action that would be. Come to one, two, or three actions that you believe would benefit you. Specify when, where, how, and with whom you will carry out these actions. Commit yourself to doing them. Rationally decide on the first steps that are needed for each, and describe them in your journal. With someone who cares about you, make a contract regarding the first steps you will take. Verbally commit yourself to specific actions you will complete this week. At the end of the week, meet with the person, discuss what occurred, and, if you wish, make a contract for the following week based on what you learned and what you know you still need to learn. Make a ritual of meeting each week, attending to the atmosphere, perhaps involving food, candles, or nature. Continue to update and renew your contract for as long as you find having a contract to be of value.

Peg's Contract

"My cries that 'I need more time' and that 'I've been a laggard scholar in terms of too many lessons of appreciation, patience, generosity, honor, mercy, humility left to learn' define my contract.

"My time is precious; I must be thoughtful, intuitive, protective, and generous in allocating it. I must keep my body healthy, having squandered much of my genetic advantage in casual disregard of its well-being. I know how to improve my ways of self-nurture, and I will allocate my time so I can make those improvements.

"I dare not hurry as a result of failing patience or out of fear of missing something. Stinginess with things or with my energy serves no purpose, but I must not be grandiose about my resources. I deserve a generous portion of my own hours. To learn my lessons, I cannot indulge in hateful cleverness or self-serving shady practices. I would be dishonorable, most of all, to myself. Compassion must not be stifled. I must give myself exposure to others' pain in order to be filled with loving-kindness, a most joyful experience. And humility. It is too easy to bask in the glow of the need of others to have me be wise—to have the illusion that I, having lived this long, know the answers. I know some of *my* answers—for right now. But the hunger to be loved has sometimes led me to the mistake of inflating myself so I feel big and in some ways 'better' than others. I must be modest from the heart, where I know that we are all part of the One, and none is greater or lesser than the other parts.

"This week I will drink fresh orange juice instead of wine; I'll hike on The Land instead of vegetating in a chair. I'll hug a neighbor rather than hiding away with my books. I'll say 'thank you' instead of 'I want.' And I'll swim each day. I will affirm these words daily:

> This is a good day to die
> The Sun will rise tomorrow

This is a good day to die
The River flows endlessly
This is a good day to die
I follow my bliss into the Earth."

Robert's Contract

"First of all, I am going to give myself some time before jumping into another two-year project. Having just completed the Larson contract, I have plenty to do without attaching heart and soul to another all-consuming commitment. I do feel I make a real contribution to the world with such projects, and there is certainly a great aesthetic satisfaction—but it costs me so much in relationship to being in the present moment. As a loin-clothed bull, sitting cross-legged and gurulike in a 'Far Side' cartoon puts it, 'Don't forget to slow down and eat the roses.'

"Putting all my striving into the context of my limited time on the planet changes my outlook about it. If I'm not totally overcommitted to performing good works, I start to feel empty and worry. I intend to *not* overcommit myself and to face the emptiness and worry straight on. Dawn has been begging me for years to shift my priorities. I will announce today that from this point onward I will consult her before taking on any new large projects, and we will talk each one through until we come to a consensus about what is best for me and for us, not just for my career.

"I will use the freed-up time and energy wisely. I have training in meditation, but I rarely meditate. I love nature, but I don't spend much time in it. I am always welcome to just lie back and play with the kids and with Dawn, but I'm always too busy. I will no longer steal from such activities to support my career goals, nor will I fill up the free time with other devices I've used in the past to avoid facing myself, such as spending endless hours writing clever computer programs. One other thing I will commit myself to doing, although it really scares me, is to find some kind of vision quest or outward-bound experience that pushes me to my limits. I'm afraid of a true 'death-rebirth' encounter, but I don't know any better way to forge into the deeper truths about who I am."

As you complete your contract and begin to implement it, you will be bringing your renewed mythology about death into life, discovering ever more deeply how your awareness of death can be a positive force. Elisabeth Kübler-Ross wrote, "Those who have the strength and the love to sit with a dying patient in the *silence that goes beyond words* will know that this moment is neither frightening nor painful. . . . Watching a peaceful death [is like watching] a falling star."[5] We hope this program has brought you into a greater sense of peace regarding your mortality, pointed the way toward a relationship with death that brings new meaning and vitality to your life, and shown you how to create personal and shared rituals that can be resources for you and your loved ones when the shadow called death enters your lives.

Notes

PREFACE

1. Stanislav Grof and Christina Grof, *Beyond Death: The Gates of Consciousness* (New York: Thames & Hudson, 1980), 7.

2. Elisabeth Kübler-Ross, *Death: The Final Stage of Growth* (Englewood Cliffs, NJ: Prentice-Hall, 1975), 1.

INTRODUCTION

1. Sogyal Rinpoche, *The Tibetan Book of Living and Dying* (San Francisco: HarperSanFrancisco, 1992), 11.

2. Edward Hoffman, *The Right to Be Human: A Biography of Abraham Maslow* (Los Angeles: Tarcher, 1988), 325.

3. Irvin D. Yalom, *Existential Psychotherapy* (New York: Basic Books, 1980).

4. From Nanci Shandera, "Midwifing Death: An Alternative Method of Working with Death and Dying," *Shaman's Drum* 14 (1988): 21.

5. Ernest Becker, *The Denial of Death* (New York: Free Press, 1973).

6. Marcel Proust, *Remembrance of Things Past* (New York: Random House, 1982).

7. For further discussion of the mythological predicament of the contemporary individual, see the epilogue of David Feinstein and Stanley Krippner, *Personal Mythology: The Psychology of Your Evolving Self* (Los Angeles: Tarcher, 1988).

8. Otto van der Hart, *Rituals in Psychotherapy: Transition and Continuity* (New York: Irvington, 1983); Gene Combs and Jill Freedman, *Symbol, Story, and Ceremony: Using Metaphor in Individual*

and Family Therapy (New York: Norton, 1990); Evan Imber-Black, Janine Roberts, and Richard Whiting, eds., *Rituals in Families and Family Therapy* (New York: Norton, 1988).

GETTING STARTED:
Your Images About Death and Its Meaning

1. David Feinstein, "Mythologies of Death and Their Evolution," in Gary Doore, ed., *What Survives? The Prospect of Life After Death* (Los Angeles: Tarcher, 1990), 255–64.

THE FIRST STAGE:
Rattling Your System of Death Denial

1. Becker, *The Denial of Death,* 19–20.
2. Yalom, 78–103.
3. Yalom, 91.
4. Yalom, 111.
5. Becker, *The Denial of Death.*
6. Yalom, 27.
7. Yalom, 163.
8. Yalom, 165.

THE SECOND STAGE:
Transcending the Fear of Death

1. Ken Wilber, *Up from Eden: A Transpersonal View of Human Evolution* (Garden City, NY: Doubleday, 1981), x.
2. Robert Jay Lifton, *The Broken Connection: On Death and the Continuity of Life* (New York: Basic Books, 1983), 35.
3. Lifton, 21.
4. Lifton, 20.
5. Lifton, 24–25.
6. William James, *Varieties of Religious Experience* (1902; reprint, New York: Crowell-Collier, 1961), 332.
7. Yalom, 188.
8. Yalom, 196.

9. Yalom, 43.

10. Yalom, 189–90.

11. Yalom, 212.

12. Yalom, 212.

13. Yalom, 212.

14. Mircea Eliade, *The Sacred and the Profane: The Nature of Religion,* trans. Willard R. Trask (New York: Harcourt, Brace & World, 1959).

THE THIRD STAGE:
A Confrontation Between the Fear of Death and Images of Transcending Death

1. Ernest Becker, *Escape from Evil* (New York: Free Press, 1975), 31.

2. Raymond A. Moody, *Life After Life* (New York: Bantam, 1976); Kenneth Ring, *Heading Toward Omega: In Search of the Meaning of the Near-Death Experience* (New York: Morrow, 1984).

3. Grof and Grof, 6.

4. Aldous Huxley, *The Perennial Philosophy* (New York: Harper & Row, 1970), vii.

5. Ring, *Heading Toward Omega.*

6. Philip Shaver, "Consciousness Without the Body," review of *Flight of Mind: A Psychological Study of the Out-of-Body Experience* and *Heading Toward Omega: In Search of the Meaning of the Near-Death Experience, Contemporary Psychology* 31 (1986): 646–47.

7. Roger Woolger, *Other Lives, Other Selves: A Jungian Psychotherapist Discovers Past Lives* (New York: Doubleday, 1987).

8. Ian Stevenson, *Children Who Remember Past Lives* (Charlottesville: University Press of Virginia, 1987).

9. Shaver, 647.

THE FOURTH STAGE:
Toward a Renewed Mythology About Death

1. Stephen Levine, *Who Dies: An Investigation of Conscious Living and Conscious Dying* (Garden City, NY: Doubleday, 1982), 200.

2. Levine, 27.

3. Levine, 26.

4. Levine, 26.

5. William Irwin Thompson, *Passages About Earth: An Exploration of the New Planetary Culture* (New York: Harper & Row, 1974), 174.

6. Case first presented in Feinstein and Krippner.

THE FIFTH STAGE:
Bringing Your Renewed Mythology About Death into Life

1. These practices were perceptively explained by Rabbi Aryeh Hirshfield of Ashland, Oregon, and his insights are gratefully acknowledged.

2. Many of these issues are raised in a valuable little book by Danielle Light called *Remembering Me: A Journal for You and Your Loved Ones* (available for $9.95 postpaid from Mt. Shasta Publications, P.O. Box 436, Mt. Shasta, CA 96067).

3. Sogyal Rinpoche, *The Tibetan Book of Living and Dying* (San Francisco: HarperSanFrancisco, 1992).

4. E. J. Gold, *American Book of the Dead*, 6th ed. (Nevada City, CA: Gateways, 1991).

5. Elisabeth Kübler-Ross, *On Death and Dying* (New York: Macmillan, 1969), 276.

Suggested Reading

Adler, C. S., G. Stanford, and S. M. Adler, eds. *We Are But a Moment's Sunlight: Understanding Death.* New York: Pocket Books, 1976.

Ashcroft-Nowicki, D. *New Book of the Dead.* London: Aquarian, 1992.

Beck, R., and S. B. Metrick. *The Art of Ritual.* Berkeley, CA: Celestial Arts, 1990.

Becker, E. *The Denial of Death.* New York: Free Press, 1973.

Bertman, S. L. *Facing Death: Images, Insights, and Interventions.* Washington, DC: Hemisphere, 1991.

Biesser, A. R. *A Graceful Passage.* Garden City, NY: Doubleday, 1990.

Boerstler, R. W. *Letting Go: A Holistic and Meditative Approach to Living and Dying.* South Yarmouth, MA: Associates in Thanatology, 1991.

Boulden, J. *Life Before Death Workbook.* Santa Rosa, CA: Boulden, 1991.

Buckman, R. *I Don't Know What to Say.* Isis, NY: ISIS, 1989.

Bugental, J. F. T. "Confronting the Existential Meaning of 'My Death' Through Group Exercises." *Interpersonal Development* 4 (1974): 148–63.

Cahill, S., and J. Halpern. *The Ceremonial Circle.* San Francisco: HarperSanFrancisco, 1990.

Carlson, L. *Caring for Your Own Dead.* Hinesburg, VT: Upper Access, 1987.

Doore, G., ed. *What Survives: The Prospect of Life After Death.* Los Angeles: Tarcher, 1990.

Duda, D. *Coming Home: A Guide to Dying at Home with Dignity.* Santa Fe, NM: Aurora, 1987.

Feifel, H. *New Meanings of Death*. New York: McGraw-Hill, 1977.

Feinstein, D. "Psychological Interventions in the Treatment of Cancer." *Clinical Psychology Review* 3 (1983): 1–14.

Feinstein, D., and S. Krippner. *Personal Mythology: The Psychology of Your Evolving Self*. Los Angeles: Tarcher, 1988.

Fortunato, J. E. *AIDS: The Spiritual Dilemma*. San Francisco: Harper & Row, 1987.

Garret-Garrison, J. G., and S. Shepherd. *Cancer and Hope*. Minneapolis: CompCare, 1989.

Gold, E. J. *American Book of the Dead*. 6th ed. Nevada City, CA: Gateways, 1991.

Greyson, B. "Near-Death Experiences and Attempted Suicide." *Suicide and Life-Threatening Behavior* 11 (1981): 17–21.

Grof, S., and C. Grof. *Beyond Death: The Gates of Consciousness*. New York: Thames & Hudson, 1980.

Grof, S., and J. Halifax. *The Human Encounter with Death*. New York: Dutton, 1977.

Grollman, E. A. *Concerning Death: A Practical Guide for the Living*. Boston: Beacon Press, 1974.

———. *Talking About Death: A Dialogue Between Parent and Child*. Boston: Beacon Press, 1990.

Grosso, M. *The Final Choice*. Walpole, NH: Stillpoint Press, 1985.

Imber-Black, E., and J. Roberts. *Rituals for Our Times: Celebrating, Healing, and Changing Our Lives and Our Relationships*. New York: HarperCollins, 1992.

Jevine, R. F., and A. Levitan. *No Time for Nonsense: Self-Help for the Seriously Ill*. San Diego: LuraMedia, 1989.

Johnson, C., and M. G. McGee, eds. *How Different Religions View Death and Afterlife*. Seattle: Charles, 1991.

Kapleau, P. *The Wheel of Life and Death: A Practical and Spiritual Guide*. Garden City, NY: Doubleday, 1989.

Kelley, P., and M. Callanan. *Final Gifts: Understanding the Special Awareness, Needs, and Communication of the Dying*. New York: Poseidon, 1992.

Kramer, K. P. *Sacred Art of Dying: How World Religions Understand Death*. Mahwah, NJ: Paulist Press, 1988.

Kübler-Ross, E. *On Death and Dying*. New York: Macmillan, 1969.

——. *Death: The Final Stage of Growth*. Englewood Cliffs, NJ: Prentice-Hall, 1975.

——. *Working It Through: An Elisabeth Kübler-Ross Workshop on Life, Death and Transcendence*. New York: Macmillan, 1982.

LeShan, L. *Cancer as a Turning Point: A Handbook for People with Cancer*. New York: Dutton, 1989.

Levine, S. *Who Dies: An Investigation of Conscious Living and Conscious Dying*. Garden City, NY: Doubleday, 1982.

——. *Meetings at the Edge*. Garden City, NY: Doubleday, 1984.

——. *Healing into Life and Death*. Garden City, NY: Doubleday, 1987.

Lifton, R. J. *The Broken Connection: On Death and the Continuity of Life*. New York: Basic Books, 1983.

Light, D. *Remembering Me: A Journal for You and Your Loved Ones*. Mount Shasta, CA: Mt. Shasta Publications, 1986.

Moody, R. A. *Life After Life*. New York: Bantam, 1976.

——. *The Light Beyond*. New York: Bantam, 1989.

Morgan, E. *Dealing Creatively with Death: A Manual of Death Education and Simple Burial*. 11th ed. Burnsville, NC: Celo, 1988.

Outerbridge, D., and A. Hersh. *Easing the Passage*. New York: HarperCollins, 1991.

Peacock, V. *Family Heritage Workbook*. 2nd ed. Missoula, MT: ScribeWrite, 1982.

Ring, K. *Heading Toward Omega: In Search of the Meaning of Near-Death Experiences*. New York: Morrow, 1984.

Rinpoche, S. *The Tibetan Book of Living and Dying*. San Francisco: HarperSanFrancisco, 1992.

Rosen, E. J. *Families Facing Death*. New York: Free Press, 1990.

Roth, D., and E. LeVier. *Being Human in the Face of Death*. Santa Monica, CA: IBS Press, 1990.

Rowe, D. *The Construction of Life and Death*. New York: Wiley, 1982.

Ruitenbeek, H. M., ed. *Death: Interpretations*. New York: Delta, 1969.

Schneidman, E. *Voices of Death*. New York: Harper & Row, 1980.

Simpson, M. A. *The Facts of Death: A Complete Guide for Being Prepared*. Englewood Cliffs, NJ: Prentice-Hall, 1979.

Sublette, K., and M. Flagg. *Final Celebrations: A Personal and Family Funeral Planning Guide*. San Bernardino, CA: Borgo, 1992.

Tada, J. E. *When Is It Right to Die?* San Francisco: HarperSanFrancisco, 1992.

Tatelbaum, J. *The Courage to Grieve*. New York: Harper & Row, 1980.

van der Hart, O., ed. *Coping with Loss: The Therapeutic Use of Leave-Taking Rituals*. New York: Irvington, 1988.

Wass, H., F. M. Berardo, and R. A. Neimeyer, eds. *Dying: Facing the Facts*. 2nd ed. Washington, DC: Hemisphere/Harper & Row, 1988.

Welch, I. D., D. W. Smart, and R. I. Zawistoski. *Encountering Death: Structured Activities for Death Awareness*. Muncie, IN: Accelerated Development, 1991.

White, J. *A Practical Guide to Death and Dying*. Wheaton, IL: Quest Books, 1988.

Yalom, I. D. *Existential Psychotherapy*. New York: Basic Books, 1980.

Index

Supplemental Programs and Materials

A cassette tape that contains the guided imagery instructions presented in *Mortal Acts,* with meditative background music, is offered for $9.95 by Innersource, a nonprofit health education organization. The album "Serenade at the Doorway," whose poignant lyrics and beautiful music provide powerful support to anyone facing death or bereavement, is available on cassette for $10.95 and on CD for $15.95. Please add $2 shipping and handling per order ($3 for overseas airmail). Send name, address, and phone number with check, money order, or credit card number to Innersource, 777 East Main Street, Ashland, OR 97520, or leave ordering information on the Innersource message tape by calling 503–482–1800. The institutional support of Innersource in the development of this volume is gratefully acknowledged. A free brochure describing other available tapes and books is included with each order or may be requested by mail or phone.